Intervening

with

Parents

OF STUDENTS
WHO ABUSE
ALCOHOL
OR OTHER DRUGS

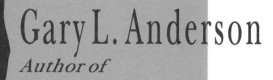

Gary L. Anderson
Author of
When Chemicals Come to School

COMMUNITY RECOVERY PRESS   PO BOX 20979   GREENFIELD, WI 53220

TABLE OF CONTENTS

AUTHOR'S PREFACE

HOW TO USE THIS BOOK

Organization

This guide is divided into three natural divisions. *Part I,* Chapters 1 through 3, discusses the prerequisites to intervening successfully: understanding the nature of the problem, understanding the nature of denial, and understanding intervention. *Part II,* Chapters 4 through 12, discusses eight discrete tasks that are essential to preparing for a successful structured intervention. Finally, the Appendices provide additional supporting information on legal issues, on how to apply this process to intervening with students as well as parents, and on how the facilitator can schedule and conduct the preparation sessions.

The person considering utilizing the process described here will find it most useful to review the materials in the order they are presented. Preparing for a successful structured intervention with parents (Chapter 12) presupposes a mastery of the preparation tasks (Chapter 4 through 11). Appreciating why certain tasks are essential, in turn, presupposes an understanding the nature of denial and its relationship to intervention.

Training

All but the alcohol and other drug abuse professional will probably hesitate to facilitate or moderate a structured intervention confrontation based solely on a reading of this book. No attempt has been made here to explain the details and complexities of student alcohol/drug abuse nor to detail those skills and techniques that are normally a part of the counselor's background. Those individuals who wish to put into practice the principles herein should acquire as much training as possible in these areas. On the other hand, alcohol and other drug abuse training alone does not make the intervention process obvious. I hope this book will spur many on to seek competent training, that it will illuminate the applications of the training that others have already received, and that it will provide the experienced interventionist with a concise and organized guide to his practice.

STUDENT ASSISTANCE PROGRAMS

Student Assistance Programs (SAP's) and Core Team processes are mentioned in several places in the text. While such programs are not essential to applying the intervention process, many of the tasks that are routine in

SAP's are also prerequisites to intervening with parents or students: identifying the troubled student, gathering preliminary assessment data, utilizing a Core Team to make appropriate recommendations for intervention, and using a combination of in-school support systems and community resources to help students to become and remain drug-free. Those who are involved in student assistance programs will find that the experience will make much of what is described here seem familiar. I hope that those who are not will find that implementing student assistance programs will provide the best context for practicing these intervention skills.

TERMINOLOGY

he/she

The reader will notice that I have avoided the use of "he/she, his/her, him/her" as singular personal pronouns. Instead, I have alternated male and female gender pronouns in each chapter. For example, masculine pronouns ("he, his") are used to refer to a student, parent, facilitator, or intervention team member in odd-numbered chapters; feminine pronouns are used in even-numbered chapters.

Alcohol and other drug abuse

Chemical dependency

Because many still do not fully appreciate that alcohol is a drug, I have used the phrase "alcohol and other drug abuse" throughout—sometimes contracted to "alcohol/drug abuse"—to refer to any type of chemical problem. Also, my own view is that *any* ingestion of alcohol or other mood-altering drugs by students is abuse. Hence, I have avoided distinguishing between "use" and "abuse." I have, however, made meaningful distinctions in the discussion between "abuse" and "chemical dependency," where the nature of the student's chemical behavior implies different courses of action.

"Parents"

Finally, the term "parents" is used throughout, as if it assumes that all students have two natural parents and is if they are living in intact, traditional families. We all know that this is not the case. In the interests of brevity I have consciously avoided qualifying each major issue with separate considerations for every racial, ethnic, linguistic, legal, psychological, and socio-economic variable which serves, today, to define "family." I have to assume that the reader knows his students and their families well, and that he will be able to extract the general principles discussed here and apply them creatively, taking into account the unique needs of each situation.

Gary L. Anderson
February, 1993

PART 1: PRELIMINARIES

Chapters 1 through 3 lay the groundwork for preparing a structured intervention.

Chapter 1: Intervening with Parents
- ❏ What circumstances require intervention?
- ❏ What have been some pitfalls to intervening successfully?

Chapter 2: Understanding Denial
- ❏ Why is denial "not a wall"?
- ❏ What functions does denial perform for parents?
- ❏ How is denial manifested in behavior?
- ❏ How does enabling relate to denial?
- ❏ What is the relationship between denial and intervention?

Chapter 3: Understanding Intervention
- ❏ What are the common types of intervention?
- ❏ What is confrontation?
- ❏ What is the preparation process for intervention with parents?

CHAPTER ONE

INTERVENING WITH PARENTS

All of you know John. He was an average student (or, he needed special programming, or he was brilliant). He had a few close friends (or, he was a loner, or he was a social leader) and was ordinary enough to be invisible (or, the staff was constantly preoccupied with his misconduct, or all the teachers wished every student could be more like him).

Whatever John *was* like, something started to happen in seventh grade. He had a morning paper route and a permit to allow him to be out before 5 am—technically a curfew violation—to deliver newspapers before going to school. He started sneaking out of the house after midnight to meet his friends and get high. If the police saw him, he just showed them his permit. By eighth grade he was sneaking out three or four nights a week, without his parents suspecting. He stopped seeing most of his old buddies and hung around with friends who would drink with him. He came to school tired, hungry, and often high. He became apathetic and inattentive in class. Some of his teachers took him aside occasionally to talk to him about his falling grades, but he explained that it was his job and "troubles at home."

By ninth grade he was missing school often, going home after his paper route in the morning—after his parents had gone to work—to watch television and sleep. He was spending a lot of time in detention for cutting classes and being tardy. At home, his parents noticed that he was gone more and more at night, and stopped keeping up his responsibilities around the house. He never ate meals with them anymore, or wanted to go to the movies or visit relatives with family members. When he was suspended from school twice, once for stealing and once for vandalism, his parents blamed it on the company he was keeping.

At home, he was physically abusive to his younger siblings. He started to drink and smoke marijuana in his room while his parents were out, and to steal or extort money from his brothers and sisters, threatening them with violence if they told. He had given up his paper route, but still went out at night after everyone was asleep (sometimes his mother heard him leave, but she had stopped saying anything about it). By now he and his friends were breaking into houses and small businesses after they got high. On one occasion he was caught by the police and his parents had to pick him up at the police station, and he was subsequently put on probation. This was just after his parents' divorce.

Then in the middle of his ninth grade year, things started to get worse. In the course of just one month he was suspended from school for being intoxicated, he was in detention for threatening a teacher, he stole a car, he was ticketed for driving under the influence, he broke up with his girlfriend and went on a four-day binge, and threatened his mother with a knife while they were arguing about her having to miss work to go to court with him.

John's decline did not go unnoticed by his family. At first they thought his tiredness was due to his morning paper route. Then they attributed his moodiness to "growing pains." It was also clear to them that he started to become more isolated and distant as soon as he started to associate with "bad company." When he began to break rules at home and at school, his parents tried whatever they could think of: at first they were understanding, then they came down hard and revoked his privileges. When his behavior didn't change, they gave that up and started arguing. The more they tried to control him, and failed, the more inadequate and frustrated they felt. There had been problems in their marriage before this, but differences over how to discipline John widened the breach between them and they began blaming each other. They knew something was wrong, but they had only the faintest idea about what it was, how long it had been going on, how deep it went, or what to do about it.

As John's behavior became more public—the school was calling, neighbors and relatives were talking, there were court appearances—they began to feel more and more ashamed. Why couldn't they control this, fix it? What did they do to make him turn out this way? What must people think of them as parents? How could their family have turned out this way? Why had everything they had hoped and dreamed for their son vanished? Why was it getting hard even to love him?

For a while, they were able to ignore telephone calls and letters from the school. When the suspensions started, they had to meet with the principal and the counselor. Despite their pain and sadness, they pretended everything was all right at home. They were always able to hide their feelings, promise to do better, or tell the school to handle its own problems with John because he was fine at home.

PITFALLS

If we, as educators, have tried to confront a student's parents and the outcome was not as we had hoped, usually it is not because of what is the matter with the student or his family, or because there is something wrong with us. Most often it is because, in intervening, so many more things can go wrong than can go right:

❏ Perhaps we confronted them alone and found ourselves outnumbered—by the parents, their denial system, and the other people in the student's environment who were tacitly enabling the behavior to continue;

❏ Perhaps we only spoke to parents in generalizations, or shared only suspicions, or reported what others have said— which they easily refuted.

❏ Perhaps we didn't have enough information: we knew about the concern of a teacher, but not about what other teachers, students, siblings, and law enforcement officers had seen.

❏ Perhaps we didn't know about the student's abuse of alcohol or other drugs, or were afraid to bring it up;

❏ Perhaps we didn't have a definite goal for the meeting—just a hope that between us we could "work something out";

❏ Perhaps our goal was inappropriate—we may have expected parents to exert control over their child when, unbeknownst us, they were feeling powerless and inadequate;

❏ Perhaps we had no consequences for the student's failure to change, or reasserted old threats;

❏ Perhaps parents caught us off guard with their objections to seeking help— *"He won't agree to go and we can't make him,"* or *"We can't afford treatment"* sounded pretty convincing;

❏ Faced with parents' resistance, perhaps we tried to argue, to convince, to out-shout long after the moment of their surrender had come and gone;

❏ Perhaps, because we thought confrontation is too painful we tried to avoid all emotion, using only logic and reason;

❏ Perhaps, when the time came to explain to parents what we wanted them to do, we gave them conflicting advice, or started debating among ourselves.

Or, worst of all, because we wrote the student and his family off, or because we feared legal liability or a lawsuit, or because we felt no one else in the school would support us, or because we had tried it and failed before—we decided to do nothing.

Intervening with parents can, however, be successful, and successful most of the time. There are things which we can do which unwittingly contribute to parents' denial, and there are ways of structuring the intervention to reduce denial. Perhaps the most important element contributing to any intervention's success will be the degree of preparation that goes into it: the confrontation with parents is not the *first* thing we do when we have a concern—it is the *last*. Also crucial to success is seeing that the object of the intervention is not the student, the parent, or "the problem," but denial.

CHAPTER TWO

UNDERSTANDING DENIAL

Something there is that doesn't love a wall,
That wants it down.
- Robert Frost, "Mending Wall"

"Denial" is a simple concept. Yet it is applied in so many contexts as to be confusing. For example, nearly everyone has an intuitive sense of its meaning, and yet the same term is often applied to an individual behavior ("rationalizing"), a general stance ("we need to confront her denial") or a global "denial system." Yet in each of these contexts "denial" indicates something quite different. Because intervention is primarily directed at the denial system, not the person, it is important to be specific about it: what it is, how it functions, and how it manifests itself.

DENIAL IS NOT A WALL...

We are often unwitting victims of our metaphors. How often have we heard, in everyday speech, or pamphlets, and even in some workshops, that someone has a "strong wall of denial," and that we won't get anywhere with them until we "break though it," or "break down their wall of denial"? Denial is often described in these terms because it is a powerful influence and often feels like a tangible presence, physical and insurmountable.

But these metaphors can be a source of the difficulties we often experience in trying to work with denial. These are metaphors that are more reflective of their user's frustrations in encountering denial than they are descriptive of what denial is. These metaphors usually result in responses to denial that attempt to "break down" or "break through." I would suggest that these violent characterizations often lead to violent, abusive, and assaultive strategies against which parents or students protect themselves. Rather than reducing denial, these approaches merely exaggerate it. (One could argue, as well, that these attitudes toward denial are part of the larger denial system itself).

A more useful characterization of denial involves accepting the validity of several principles. First, everyone (parents, kids, ourselves) is doing the best they can with what they know, or with the resources they currently have. The pain and problems caused by drug abuse and chemical dependency are issues against which students and families struggle interminably. Their failure to change successfully, despite the pain, is evidence that outside help is needed. Secondly, to the extent that parents or students fully appreciate what is happening to them, they will know what they need to do to change. Pains clearly felt usually result in appropriate steps to stop it. Third, since parents rarely admit spontaneously that their child has a serious problem, it must be because they lack vital information. A number of factors, however, conspire to keep parents from really knowing what is going on: things like suppression, defense mechanisms, fear, or their child's secretiveness, or the failure of the school to supply them with appropriate information. Finally, the above implies that denial is not a "wall" that needs to be "broken down," but a deficit that needs to be remedied.

Denial is not a wall to be broken down

Denial defined

Denial, then, can be defined as *the failure of an individual (or student, family, or school) to fully appreciate the nature, scope, and implications of a "problem."* As such, denial consists of all of those factors that operate to impair the person's awareness ("appreciation") of what is happening. Denial is something to be reduced; awareness is something to be enhanced. Let us look at the definition more closely.

First, "fully appreciate" is used in the broadest sense possible. For "appreciate" understand "grasp, know, see, hear, feel, understand, assimilate, integrate, etc." Denial consists of facts a person does not know, has repressed, suppressed, or forgotten. It consists of feelings, usually painful, which have been pushed out of awareness by ego defenses. It consists of patterns that have not been seen because individual episodes have been "put behind us." It consists, also, of cognitive knowledge that the person or family lacks concerning drug abuse and dependency, enabling, and denial. It consists of information that others have which has been unspoken or hidden. If a family could have access to all of this, the decision to take difficult steps would become inescapable.

Second, parents are frequently unaware of the "nature" of their child's problem: that it is related to the abuse of alcohol or other drugs. Even if parents are aware of chemical abuse they may see the drug behavior as a symptom of something else. In fact, drug abuse either *causes* problems, *aggravates* existing problems, or *prevents* their successful resolution. The more accurate "nature" of the problem, then, is that drug abuse is itself a problem or is causing problems. In other cases, where chemical dependency is suspected, parents typically do not know that chemical dependency is an illness by nature: that it is primary, progressive, chronic, and ultimately fatal. Grasping, to some extent, the nature of chemical dependency leads to different courses of action. In other words, some parents may not know that their child is abusing alcohol and other drugs; others may know of the abuse but are unaware of its implications for resolving problems; still others may know of the abuse but may not appreciate that it is possible that their child is chemically dependent.

Third, even if they grasp the nature of the problem, parents will typically be unaware of the true scope of their student's alcohol and other drug abuse and its associated problems. They may only have observed a few incidents, or none at all. They do not have access to the information possessed by other family members, the school system, their child's friends or friends' parents, etc. They may know that their child drinks but other drug involvement is hidden. They will also lack information about how long it has been going on or that it is worsening: usually, a teenager has been abusing chemicals for a long time before obvious signs appear.

Finally, even if parents know that their child is abusing alcohol or other drugs, and that it is a primary problem which must itself be addressed, they may not appreciate the implications for courses of action. At the least, many parents do not understand or agree with the view that abstinence is the goal: *any* pattern of drug abuse actually or potentially impairs health, growth, and development. Many will excuse some drug abuse as "normal." Others may not understand the factors that support drug abuse, from peer pressure to enabling, and that achieving abstinence goes beyond "just say no." And most will not understand that the implication of chemical dependency is treatment.

Denial, then, can be defined as the failure of an individual (or student, family, or school) to fully appreciate the nature, scope, and implications of a "problem."

In short, then, our task is not to "break through" denial but to supply parents (or others) with information of many types, the lack of which prevents them fully appreciating the nature, scope, and implications of their student's alcohol or other drug abuse. A prerequisite for working with the denial in others is to have as complete a picture as possible ourselves of the nature, scope, and implications of the problem.

THE FUNCTIONS OF DENIAL

Denial, regardless of its specific form, exists and persists and has the strength that it does because it works: it performs some function or addresses some need for the parents or student (Gorski , p. 3). We need to understand what it accomplishes for parents; in confronting denial, we need to utilize strategies that meet these same needs in healthier ways.

Denial works because it functions to protect self-worth, self-esteem, and self-respect. Parents frequently blame themselves, at some level, for the patterns of misbehavior in their teenagers. And, where drug abuse and chemical dependency are involved, the social stigma that still attaches to these problems makes them even more difficult to acknowledge. Furthermore, the immediate response of parents to the telephone call from the school— that their child has a problem—is self-protection: protecting the family's image before a public institution. Denial, regardless of its form, allows parents to think that they are still "OK."

Denial also *makes reality appear to be manageable.* The teenager with a serious problem with alcohol or other drugs will eventually become unmanageable. His behavior fails to respond to rules, limits, or punishments by parents, the school, or the community. His drug abuse itself may be out of control. Serious patterns of misbehavior lead parents to fear the loss of their dreams for their child or for their family. By denying the nature of the problem (drug abuse) or its seriousness, parents are still able to maintain the fiction that life still makes sense.

Thus, denial also *functions to provide parents a mythical sense of control* over a situation that is out of control. The more out of control their child's behavior, the greater a parent's attempts to control it. Part of the denial consists of failing to see the difference between control and influence over another's behavior.

Finally, denial *provides parents with mythical solutions to problems.* Failing to see drug abuse itself as a problem, many parents will adopt strategies to address what they see as its causes: having more rules, having fewer rules, changing schools, trying to affect with whom their child associates, punishing, rewarding, and so on.

MANIFESTATIONS OF DENIAL

In general terms, denial consists of an absence of information, a failure to "fully appreciate" what is happening. It is also a phenomenon that benefits people, even though these are only apparent benefits. Specifically, though, what are the factors that impair awareness, and how do these present themselves to us?

Ego Defenses We tend to encounter denial most frequently through "defensiveness," or the rigid, practiced employment of ego defenses in threatening circumstances. An ego defense can be defined as a spontaneous response to a feeling (usually painful) that blocks the individual's awareness of that feeling. Ego defenses, like denial in general, function to protect self-esteem, self-worth, self-concept, self-image. Ego defenses can be seen as normal, natural human strategies for self-protection to the extent that they are used choicefully and with full awareness. To the extent that ego defenses are employed repeatedly, unconsciously, and choicelessly they tend to impair awareness of feelings and block healthy responses to those feelings as well as to the situations that produce them.

For example, suppose that you are at a meeting where your supervisor says something that makes you angry. You might acknowledge to yourself how you are feeling, but decide not to respond or express that feeling now out of self-protection. You might, instead, decide to express your anger in private, with trusted others. On the other hand, someone else might respond to anger with blaming and hostility—i.e., defensively—because they habitually have always done so. The response is choiceless and compulsive; it may also be self-destructive to react this way to one's supervisor.

Functions of Denial

❏ Denial allows parents to maintain self-esteem and self-worth

❏ Denial makes reality seem manageable

❏ Denial provides a mythical sense of control over problems

❏ Denial provides mythical solutions to problems

The behavior also prevents the person from acknowledging their own anger or the hurt that lies beneath it, and so prevents resolving that issue.

When confronting parents we typically encounter defensiveness: the use of ego defenses that have been practiced so long in response to painful events as to become automatic, choiceless, and compulsive. These defenses have allowed parents, for many years, to avoid painful feelings regarding their child's behavior. Without access to these emotions, it will be nearly impossible for them to acknowledge that there is "a problem" on any meaningful level.

Defenses commonly take a number of forms. Some defense mechanisms masquerade as reason and logic. Intellectualizing, analyzing, and rationalizing function to divert a person's attention from her emotional distress by focussing on abstractions. Other defenses are more assaultive: arguing, being sarcastic, blaming. These not only divert the subject's attention from her pain, but often cause a confronter to back away. Some people respond to emotional distress by appearing calm and agreeable: joking, being compliant, being complimentary, talking a lot, or rescuing others. And still others will passively reject situations that are painful by being silent, by emotionally withdrawing, or by physically leaving the room. (Figure 2.1 presents some of the most common defenses and some representative examples.) Such defense mechanisms, arising automatically, have a dual function: they not only block the individual's awareness of painful feelings, but they can divert any interaction away from topics that are distressing. They divert my attention from my feelings, and they deflect you from pursuing a confrontation that reminds me of them.

Repression Repression is a psychological response to events that are highly traumatizing. Events which threaten one's psychological or physical well-being will often be *automatically* pushed out of consciousness. We increasingly hear examples of parents who are physically beaten by their adolescents; parents who have had to go to emergency rooms for kids involved in car accidents; parents who have been threatened with weapons for interfering with a drug deal, etc. Events like these can be too painful to acknowledge fully, and so they are "forgotten" almost immediately due to repression. While repression is typically unconscious—individuals do not know that they are repressing painful episodes—suppression is the deliberate attempt to push painful events out of awareness. When parents have said to them-

Figure 2.1

COMMON EGO DEFENSES

Defense Mechanism	Examples of Parent Comments or Behaviors	How we may see the parent who employs these defenses habitually
Intellectualizing	"Drug use has always been a part of western civilization"	Cool
		Rigid
Analyzing	"There's difference between his problems in Ms. Smith's class and how he gets along at home"	Arrogant
		Condescending
		Aloof
Rationalizing	"I think he drinks because he has low self-esteem"	Unrealistic
		Shallow
Justifying	"Kids have a right to have some fun, take some chances"	Distant
		Intellectual
Debating	"I don't think every kid should look and act the same"	Controlled
		Unfeeling
Explaining	"She fell asleep in class because she was out late babysitting"	
Minimizing	"It's not as bad as you're making it out to be."	
Generalizing	"Everybody does it now and then"	
Questioning	"If his grades are OK why are you bothering us about a little drinking?"	
Excusing	"She has had a hard time since her dad left us," " I smoked marijuana all through law school, and look how I turned out"	

Arguing	"How do you know the drugs in his locker were his?"	Hot-tempered
		Negative
Intimidating	"I have a friend on the school board"	Hostile
Threatening	"I'll sue"	Critical
Blaming	"If you kept the pushers out of this school my kid wouldn't be in this mess"	Angry
		Judgemental
Attacking	(Name-calling)	Defiant
Belittling	"All the kids say you're the worst principal in this school system"	Defensive
Criticizing	"It all started when you wouldn't let her drop algebra"	
Glaring		
Physical violence	(Fist-pounding, etc.)	

Figure 2.1

COMMON EGO DEFENSES, CONTINUED

Defense Mechanism	Examples of Parent Comments or Behaviors	How we may see the parent who employs these defenses habitually
Complying	"We'll make sure he gets here every day on time"	Compliant
Agreeing	"Whatever you say" (If I agree with everybody, there won't be any conflict)	Phony Manipulative Insincere
Stalling	"Let's wait a few weeks and see if things turn around"	Fragile "Nice guy"
Joking	"Most kids spill more than he drinks"	Weak
Equivocating	"He's given us some problems at home, but he's basically a good kid"	Wishy-washy
Complimenting	"You do such a good job of handling all these problems."	
Flattering	"All the kids say they wish you were their counselor instead of Mr. Jones."	
Talking a lot	(to prevent others from bringing up more problems)	
Rescuing	"Don't cry," "Don't get upset," "Don't worry, everything will be all right"	
Nodding Smiling	(agreeing)	

Distracting	"I think we need more police in the schools"	Depressed Sad
Avoiding	"It was so hard to get here through all the traffic"	Tired Lonely
Silence	('If I don't pay attention, none of it is true')	Scared Shy
Withdrawing Leaving Day dreaming		Uncaring

Suppression selves "That's all behind us now," or "I don't want to think about that" they have been suppressing. The net effect of both repression and suppression is that important data is lost to awareness—facts which, if the parent could have access to them in the here-and-now—would be overwhelmingly convincing of the nature, scope, and implications of a problem.

Euphoric Recall "Euphoric recall" also colors a parent's awareness: remembering only the positive aspects of an incident, or remembering one's adolescent as she used to be: "But she was always such a diligent student," or "He was always so popular and friendly," or "There wasn't anything that kid couldn't do." When parents are remembering their teenager euphorically, they are unable to see her as she is now. Facts that are inconsistent with their "rose-colored glasses" image are excluded from awareness.

Loss of Perspective Families reacting to the problems caused by drug abuse or chemical dependency frequently lose their sense of history. They learn to react—to cope—on a crisis-to-crisis basis. When a crisis arises, the family's resources are mobilized to resolve it and things return to whatever has become normal until the next crisis. Thus, parents often lose their sense of history: that their child was not always this way, that things have changed dramatically, that things are getting worse, and that all of their attempts to control it have failed. Instead, what is present in memory is only the last crisis, the last weekend drinking episode, the last suspension from school, or the last arrest.

Personal histories We know that chemical dependency has a strong genetic predisposition and that it runs in families. The chances are better than even that a chemically dependent adolescent lives in a family where one or both parents is chemically dependent or is an adult child of a chemically dependent grandparent. Where parents have alcohol and other drug problems themselves they will be unable to see their child's drug abuse as a problem. Moreover, just the physical action of drugs on the brain will impair any parent's awareness of what is happening with her child. Similarly, the denial system that evolves as one grows up in a chemically dependent family will reduce a parent's ability to see drug abuse clearly in her current family.

Absence of information Finally, simply the absence of accurate, factual information concerning alcohol and other drug abuse contributes to denial. Many parents do not see alcohol as a drug, for example. Many parents will excuse alcohol or other drug abuse as a "normal" part of "kids-will-be-kids" experimenting. Others will see drug abuse primarily in physiological terms: their students is not using drugs heavily enough to cause harm, or is not using "addict-ing" drugs. Most will not sufficiently appreciate the subtle but long-lasting effects of drug abuse on psychosocial development. Many parents will, at some point, need some factual information if they are to define their child's drug abuse as a problem. Moreover, where the school suspects chemical dependency, it frequently must teach parents that chemical dependency is an illness that is primary, progressive, chronic, and ulti-mately fatal, and that these aspects of the illness dictate clear patterns of response.

ENABLING AND DENIAL

The contribution of enabling to the denial system is not appreciated fully enough. One definition describes enabling as "those beliefs, feelings, attitudes and behaviors which unwittingly allow drug problems to continue or worsen by preventing the drug user from experiencing the consequences of his/her condition, in order to enhance, maintain, or promote the enabler's sense of well-being" (Anderson, p. 78). The drug abusing student is often protected from experiencing the consequences of her behavior by both the school system and the family. Harmful consequences that are minimized deprive her of information she will need to define her drug abuse as a problem for her.

We can substitute "family" for "drug abuser" in the definition above to see how enabling can reduce parents' awareness of what is happening. To the extent that the school, well-meaning friends, or law enforcement, for example, minimize consequences for the family, it is also deprived of information it needs to see what is happening accurately. Within the school context, reducing denial within the family system will often involve attention to three spheres of enabling:

- ❏ Reducing the school's enabling of the student, so she will experience more fully the consequence of her drug abuse;

- ❏ Reducing the school's enabling of parents, by allowing them to experience the consequences of their child's behavior;

- ❏ Reducing the enabling of parents, by giving them information about enabling and helping them to reduce it.

IMPLICATIONS

From this brief discussion of denial we can see that although it is a powerful and thorough impairment of awareness it is not a "wall" that we assault with violence. A parent's denial is not overcome with better arguments, louder voices, or stronger threats. Working with denial requires that we appreciate that it is a response to painful situations that has evolved over a considerable period of time, that is made up of many components, and that we must respect the function that it serves. Reducing denial will also require that we design a strategy that will address these various aspects of the denial system. In the following chapters we will be examining a response to denial that takes into account these factors.

To summarize: An effective response to denial:

- ❏ will ask "what do parents need to be *aware* of that they are not?
- ❏ will clearly spell out the *nature* of the problem
- ❏ will clearly delineate the *scope* of the problem
- ❏ will clearly define the *implications* of the problem
- ❏ will avoid threatening parents' self-esteem

❏ will show parents how to manage the problem successfully
❏ will empower parents to influence their child rather than trying to control her
❏ will provide a realistic solution

*Denial,
Obstruction,
and Resistance*

Finally, we have a tendency to see everything that blocks our efforts as "denial." Every "no" is not a denial. It is important to distinguish denial from "obstruction" and "resistance." *Denial,* we have said, is a failure to see accurately what is happening due to an impaired awareness system. It is a complex of intellectual, psychological, and emotional factors. *Obstruction,* on the other hand, is more tangible. Obstructions are real-world, solvable obstacles. If a parent says "We can't afford treatment," she may be right. The appropriate response to obstruction is to anticipate it and to prepare solutions. *Resistance* is a different phenomenon still. While "denial" is a statement about an individual, "resistance" is a statement about a relationship. Resistance takes two. If we resist another's denial we strengthen it.

Implicit in this discussion is the notion that we often react to a parent's denial with our own. Virtually everything that has been said about parents applies equally to many of us in the school setting—or to the school as an institution—as we try to intervene. Thus, we attempt to confront without a clear definition of the nature, scope, and extent of the problem. Or, we get "hooked" by the defenses we encounter in our meetings with parents: we debate, blame, become silent, or back down from our recommendations as we encounter those forms of denial which trigger our own. In the vast majority of cases, the success of intervening with parents depends crucially on how well we understand their patterns of denial and on how well we reduce our own.

☞ Everyone is doing the best they can with what they know or with the resources they currently have.

☞ To the extent that parents or students fully appreciate what is happening to them, they will know what they need to do to change.

☞ Denial is not a "wall" to be broken down; it is a deficit that needs to be remedied.

☞ Denial consists of all those factors that impair a person's awareness of what is happening to them.

☞ Change is possible when denial is reduced.

☞ Denial is reduced by enhancing awareness.

CHAPTER THREE

UNDERSTANDING INTERVENTION

Intervention is not about "the problem."
It is about denial.

Where chemical dependency or severe alcohol and other drug abuse are involved, the progression is inevitably downward: an ever-worsening spiral of harmful consequences. These harmful consequences of drug abuse impair the student in every area of his life: school, family relationships, the law, health, peer relationships, and healthy growth and development in general. Parents are also enmeshed in a similar downward spiral of feelings and behavior. They become increasingly frustrated; they feel increasingly powerless and inadequate; their self-esteem deteriorates; they feel more and more angry about what is happening.

To "intervene" means to "occur or to come between two things." When we intervene with a student, for example, the intervention is designed to "come between" the student and his drug abuse. More generally, the intervention strategy is designed to "occur between" the student's illness and his recovery process. Similarly, an intervention with parents is designed to come between two things: (1) the patterns of denial, enabling, and dysfunction in which they are enmeshed, and (2) a process of constructive action that leads to their own and their child's recovery. The nature of this intervention is what determines its outcome.

The pre-eminent outcome of a successful intervention strategy or process is for someone, the "object" of the intervention, to take a concrete step in the direction of health. Parents of troubled youth rarely take such steps early in the progression of problems. Spontaneous insight into the nature, scope and implications of these problems rarely occurs by itself. The denial system, as we have seen, is responsible for parents' inability to see reality clearly and to take appropriate actions.

TYPES OF INTERVENTION

"Hitting Bottom"

If intervention in a family's pattern of drug abuse or dependency occurs, it tends to happen in one three ways. The first is often called "hitting bottom." When the harmful consequences and crises caused by drug abuse become so frequent, severe, and inescapable, the denial system is overwhelmed briefly enough for the student and/or his family to take steps. Waiting for the student and his family to "hit bottom" is not the most desirable intervention strategy for many reasons. The pattern of negative consequences, which may need to evolve over many years, can be so severe as to permanently scar the student physically, intellectually, socially, emotionally, etc. Moreover, there is no guarantee that "hitting bottom" will result in the student and his family seeking *appropriate* treatment: many students will flee this painful environment ("geographic escapes"); some parents will kick their children out of their house; and many teenagers will die from their drug abuse or its consequences before appropriate help can be given.

Raising the Bottom

In a real sense it is true that until an individual "hits bottom" he will not accept help. On the other hand, it is neither wise nor necessary for us to wait until this happens by itself. The second way in which intervention can occur can be called "raising the bottom" through reduced enabling. In this case, most of the significant people in the environment become involved in allowing the student to experience the natural, logical consequences of his drug abuse. By clearly delineating his responsibilities and our expectations, and by clearly imposing consequences on his failure to act responsibly, the student gradually encounters his powerlessness and his need for help in changing his behavior.

Student assistance programs

The school, through student assistance programs, is often the most effective manager of this intervention process (see Anderson (1988), pp. 177-193). Through a combination of policy enforcement, support groups, counseling, behavioral contracting, parenting education for the family, and networking with youth services agencies, the student is allowed to experience the chain of crises which his behavior is creating. This process does not allow dozens of drug-related crises, and their damage, to pass unacknowledged. It 'raises the bottom' by forcing the student to face each crisis, and it escalates the consequences of drug abuse as each consequence occurs (See Schaefer (1987), pp. 71-119). Parent involvement is implicit in this incremental crisis management approach. We often intervene with parent denial gradually, by exploiting each instance of student misconduct as an opportunity to work with parents: supplying them with information about alcohol and other drug abuse, denial, enabling; enlisting their support in establishing clear rules and enforcing them at home; enlisting their active involvement in monitoring behavioral contracts; assisting them in acquiring parenting skills, and so on.

Structured Intervention

Third, there are times when either the student's or the parents' denial will be so strong, or the consequences of drug abuse will be so serious as to require more concerted intervention. Parents are functioning with a different "world view." Their denial system, which limits their awareness, forces them to see reality in a different way than we do. A structured intervention is a confrontation designed to supply them with the information they lack, by caring participants who present the information in a way that can be heard. In a "structured intervention" approach a crisis is precipitated through a structured confrontation. This is the strategy we will be concentrating upon.

Definition

One of the principles we advanced earlier is that to the extent that individuals fully and accurately grasp what is happening to them they will know what they need to do to change. The denial system is the set of factors which reduce this awareness. Intervention can be defined as *"a process designed to reduce the denial system to the point where an individual can grasp what he needs to do in order to change."* A structured intervention with parents is designed to help them appreciate accurately the nature, scope, and implications of their child's problem so they will know what they need to do to change. The nature of this confrontation is determined generally by guidelines for confrontation and specifically by the nature of denial.

Confrontation: "Facing Together"

☞ 1. We confront discrepancies.
☞ 2. We confront behavior, not a person.
☞ 3. We confront with facts.
☞ 4. We confront with care and concern.
☞ 5. We confront behavior parents can realistically change.
☞ 6. We confront only if we are willing to become more deeply involved.

CONFRONTATION

A structured intervention is thus designed to reduce denial through confrontation. Just as denial is not a wall, confrontation is not a crash. To confront means "to face together." A successful structured intervention is based on our observance of six rules for confrontation in general:

1. A confrontation addresses discrepancies. We decide to confront because we are aware of a marked discrepancy between *what we know* and *what parents appear to know*. Our sense is that if parents had access to all of the information we have about their student, they would willingly accede to our request that they seek help for him. Given what we understand of the denial system, we are also confronting, or facing together, reality and parents' distorted view of it.

2. Confrontation is directed at a behavior, not at a person. If a person feels that he is the subject of the confrontation, he will defend himself against a perceived personal threat. The denial system, or the various absences in parents' awareness, is what we are "facing together."

3. We confront with facts. Facts are concrete, specific, describable. The data we confront with must not be hearsay, rumors, opinions, or generalizations. Describing what others have said sounds conspiratorial. Rumors and hearsay are easily deflected ("Who said that?"), and generalizations invite debate or are not impactful. There is a clear difference in immediacy between *"Johnny is a problem in class"* and *"In my class last week, Johnny threw objects at another student, fell asleep, and tore up another student's homework."*

4. We confront with care and concern. One of the major functions of denial is to protect self-worth. Parents need to feel adequate as individuals and as parents. The family unit also needs to feel self-worth. Anything that appears to threaten these basic needs for esteem will enhance denial. Confrontation must be done in a manner that both avoids threatening self-esteem and seeks to enhance it.

5. Confrontation addresses behaviors the person can realistically change. This entails having a goal defined in advance, and it is a goal that parents can accomplish. Rather than laying out facts and then asking parents what they are going to do about them, we suggest a concrete course of action. "We would like you to take your son in for a chemical dependency evaluation" is asking for a step that parents can take.

> *Intervention can be defined as "a process designed to reduce the denial system to the point where an individual can grasp what he needs to do in order to change."*

6. Finally, confrontation is personal: only those who are willingly to become more deeply involved should participate in a confrontation. When confronted appropriately, parents feel cared about and supported. They sense that we have the best interests of their child and their family at heart. And, they understand that we will be providing any support we can for them and their student in taking the appropriate steps.

THE PROCESS

The single most important variable in predicting the successful outcome of a structured intervention is preparation. There are a number of questions that need to be answered, or tasks that need to be carried out, before anyone should conduct an intervention meeting with parents.

1. Deciding when an intervention is called-for. Under what circumstances is a formal intervention appropriate? The emotional power of a structured intervention is seldom necessary when parents are open to the school's recommendations, are cooperative, or are motivated to seek help. Decid-

Intervention Preparation Tasks

- ❑ 1. Deciding when to intervene
- ❑ 2. Identifying the intervention team
- ❑ 3. Educating the intervention team
- ❑ 4. Collecting and pooling data
- ❑ 5. Deciding on an appropriate goal
- ❑ 6. Deciding on consequences
- ❑ 7. Unhooking
- ❑ 8. Planning the agenda

ing when to utilize this process involves considering the seriousness of the student's alcohol/drug abuse, the success of his past efforts to deal with it, and the likelihood that the student and parents will follow through with recommendations for assessment and/or treatment without the formal power of the intervention.

2. Determining who will be involved. Those involved in the intervention meeting should have first-hand experience with the troubled student's behaviors of concern. In addition, intervenors who have a special relationship to the student or to parents are often useful: coaches, club advisors, a favorite teacher, etc. Counselors and support group leaders who have worked with the student and/or the family previously will also be useful, as will the principal, who can speak to disciplinary and school policy issues.

3. Educating the intervention team. Members of the intervention team need to be schooled in two key areas before intervening. They should have a basic understanding of alcohol and other drug abuse issues (e.g., drug abuse and chemical dependency, denial, enabling, etc.) and they should understand the broad outlines of the intervention process they will be engaged in.

4. **Collecting and pooling data**. What will ultimately be shared with parents are the specific facts the school has gathered that point to a need for help. The data needs to be gathered in advance and evaluated for its appropriateness. The nature and amount of specific data the school develops is what lends legitimacy to the entire intervention process.

5. Deciding on a goal. The goal of the intervention consists of the specific step the school wants parents to take, or the action it wishes parents to support. It must be clear and justified by the data. Everyone on the intervention team must be unanimous in agreeing to support the same goal.

6. Deciding on consequences. There will be consequences for the student's failure to change his behavior. These may include, for example, loss of privileges at school, problems with grades or credits toward graduation, or expulsion for the next violation of school policies. There may also be consequences for the parents if they refuse to support the need for formal treatment or care. Such consequences must be clearly defined in advance, and everyone on the intervention team needs to be aware of them.

7. "Unhooking," or becoming emotionally adequate to intervene. Many structured intervention confrontations fail because intervenors get "hooked" by the patterns of defensiveness and denial they experience in parents: a parent's blaming is countered by a defense of the school; a parent's rationalizing is met with counter-arguments, etc. These patterns of resistance serve only to divert the team or one of its members from the primary task. Anticipating how parents might react, anticipating our reactive patterns, and preparing more effective responses is a key step in intervention preparation.

8. Planning the intervention meeting agenda. The intervention meeting should not proceed accidently. While no meeting ever goes exactly as planned, a clear, predetermined structure and agenda gives team members something known to depart from and something to return to. Defining this agenda in advance, and assuring that all team members will adhere to it is also a key planning step.

PART II: PREPARATION

In Part II we examine the single most important factor in predicting the success of a structured intervention: the process of preparing members of the intervention team for the intervention meeting with parents. Chapters 4 through 11 examine each of eight preparation tasks in detail:

Chapter 4: Deciding When to Intervene
- ❑ What triggers the decision to intervene with parents?
- ❑ What is the role of a Core Team process in the decision?
- ❑ Who decides: what is the role of the intervention facilitator?

Chapter 5: Identifying the Intervention Team
- ❑ What makes someone eligible to be part of the intervention team?
- ❑ Who are some representative intervention team members?

Chapter 6: Educating the Intervention Team
- ❑ What do members of the team need to know about drug abuse?
- ❑ What do team members need to know about the process?

Chapter 7: Collecting and Pooling Data
- ❑ What are the characteristics of useful data for intervention?
- ❑ What is the facilitator's role in reviewing data?

Chapter 8: Deciding on a Goal for the Intervention
- ❑ What are appropriate and inappropriate goals?
- ❑ What are some typical intervention goals?

Chapter 9: Unhooking
- ❑ How does the team respond to parents' objections to getting help?
- ❑ How do team members avoid becoming "hooked" by parents' denial?
- ❑ What if parents refuse to get help?

Chapter 10: Deciding on Consequences
- ❑ What are effective and ineffective consequences?
- ❑ What will happen if the student fails to change his behavior?
- ❑ What will happen if parents refuse to seek help for their child?

Chapter 11: Planning the Meeting
- ❑ Who conducts the intervention meeting?
- ❑ What is the agenda for the meeting?
- ❑ How do we get parents to attend the intervention meeting?

CHAPTER FOUR

DECIDING WHEN TO INTERVENE

The structured intervention technique is a powerful tool that should be employed only after careful consideration. In general, structured intervention is justified when two circumstances converge: (1) there is a legitimate concern for the student's continued use of alcohol or other drugs, and (2) parents have thus far been unwilling or unable to support getting appropriate help, within the school or in the community. Parent intervention is most often not the first step to take on behalf of the student or her family. Rather, it becomes an option after a number of other strategies have failed to bring about the desired goal.

THE DECISION TO RECOGNIZE

Planning a structured intervention with parents is triggered by a "decision to recognize:" literally, deciding to see what has been happening with a student and her family. This decision to recognize, typically unfolding over time, is made up of five realizations:

1. *Defining alcohol and other drug abuse as a primary problem* for the student. "Primary" does not mean *causal* or *most important*. It means seeing that drug abuse is itself a problem, and that unless the student stops abusing, her problems are likely to continue.

2. *Drug abuse is a pattern.* One episode of drug abuse does not, by itself, typically justify a structured intervention. There will have been multiple episodes of abuse and associated harmful consequences of some degree.

3. *It is not getting better;* it may be getting worse. There is tendency to unconsciously lower our expectations when students exhibit patterns of unacceptable behavior. There is also a tendency to respond to one crisis at a time. Just as the family loses perspective, school staff may forget that the latest drug-related episode is not solitary but part of a growing pattern.

4. *Our previous attempts to stop it have failed.* The various strategies brought to bear upon the student's school performance and/or chemical abuse has not succeeded in bringing about significant periods of continuous abstinence or improvement. Or, up to now the school has been unable to increase the student's motivation to stay drug-free.

5. *We need the help of others.* As long as we keep doing what we have been doing with respect to a problem, the result will always be the same. The "we need help" realization often entails the realization that the student can no longer benefit from in-school services, and that parent cooperation is needed to bring about a successful referral to outside programs. "I need help" can also mean that the efforts of the individual counselor have not succeeded and the help of others is now necessary.

Thus, the decision to utilize a structured intervention with parents entails examining three areas: (1) the nature and scope of the student's alcohol/drug-related problems, (2) the steps that the school has taken thus far to correct the situation, and (3) the degree of parent denial.

STUDENT TRIGGERS

What is the nature and scope of the student's alcohol and other drug abuse?

For the student, abstinence is always the ultimate goal. Where a student appears to be chemically dependent, abstinence is the only recourse of merit, and formal treatment outside of the school system is almost always necessary. Abstinence is also the goal for students who lie elsewhere along the continuum of alcohol and other drug abuse. For these students, some combination of school-based strategies is usually successful. A structured intervention is often necessary to secure the parents' support and active involvement in the student's participation in either school-based or treatment-based programs. In short, intervention is most effective after considerable data about the student has been collected, and when the student has failed to change in response to casual, non-treatment strategies.

Thus, a facilitator might conclude that a structured intervention with parents is required, based on the needs of the student. The following considerations usually justify a formal intervention process:

☛ 1. There are *"behaviors of concern:"* specific behavioral indicators of a problem. Grades, classroom conduct, disciplinary infractions or policy violations, absenteeism, tardiness: these and other behaviors indicate that something is wrong. Furthermore, the school has data from several sources that legitimize its concern: the concern does not come from just one individual.

☛ *2. There is evidence of alcohol and/or other drug abuse.* Student alcohol and other drug abuse is complex. Patterns of drug abuse range from casual, infrequent, and light abuse to chemical dependency. Regardless of the pattern of a student's drug behavior, drug abuse is related to student problems in one or more of the following ways. First, drug abuse may be **causing** the problems in a student's life–in school, at home, and in the community. Second, drug abuse may be **aggravating** unrelated problems the student has. A student might be using alcohol or other drugs to medicate feelings of low self-esteem, or to help her cope with a number of stressors in her life. Third, drug abuse may be **preventing the student from solving problems**, or may be interfering with the efforts of others–parents, school counselors, or therapists–to help her.

☛ *3. In some cases, the school has evidence of chemical dependency.* Chemical dependency is a life-threatening, progressive illness. In these instances, formal treatment in the community is the only recourse. In any case, continued alcohol/drug abuse will compromise the student's efforts to improve school performance problems identified in (1), above. Thus, any evidence of alcohol/drug use may justify a structured intervention with parents: whether a student appears to be chemically dependent or not will only help to determine its goal (see Chapter 8).

☛ *4. It is unlikely that the student will **seek** professional help*, assessment, or treatment without the involvement and support of parents.

☛ *5. It is unlikely that the student will **remain** in treatment* or follow through with other recommendations without the involvement and support of parents.

SCHOOL—BASED TRIGGERS

What steps has the school taken thus far?

The failure of the student to change her behavior in response to strategies the school has tried can also contribute to the decision to intervene with parents. Within the context of a student assistance program process, the school may have attempted to intervene in the student's alcohol and other drug abuse through "progressive intervention" (Anderson (1988), pp. 178-186). Seen as a process, progressive intervention consists of various services offered to the student over time. At each stage, if she fails to eliminate her drug abuse or to improve her school performance, she experiences a stronger level of intervention.

Progressive intervention continuum

Students who are unwilling or unable to change their drug behavior in response to any step are indicating that their relationship to drugs is strong enough to justify a more concerted step.

Some typical components of the progressive intervention continuum include:

☛ 1. *Accurate Information.* Many students are able to stop abusing alcohol or other drugs in response to didactic information alone. Information is most often presented through classroom curricula, one-to-one counseling sessions, or support groups.

☛ 2. *Personal Consequences.* Many students will not change their drug behavior until they experience the direct consequences of their abuse. Suspensions, loss of privileges, and other disciplinary consequences reduce the enabling that may have been allowing the student to continue to abuse.

☛ 3. *Counseling for Behavioral Change.* Students who continue to abuse alcohol or other drugs are demonstrating a stronger relationship with chemicals requiring more stringent intervention. Counseling, through one-to-one sessions or use-focussed support groups can be successful in helping these students to achieve abstinence. These strategies offer awareness-enhancing opportunities for students to discuss and examining their own drug-related behavior in a safe and confidential setting. Behavior contracts are often utilized to help students live up to basic expectations for abstinence and acceptable school performance. Counseling is also designed to provide students with skills in decision-making, peer-refusal, problem-solving, etc.

☛ 4. *Family Involvement.* The school is limited in the degree to which it can require behavioral changes and monitor the student's compliance or progress. At some point, involving the family becomes necessary. The family may need help in establishing a clear expectation of abstinence, defining and imposing consequences for drug abuse or other unacceptable behaviors, and jointly monitoring the student's progress with school staff. Many students who have continued to abuse alcohol or other drugs up to this point will respond to this degree of consistent, accurate supervision and support by both the school and parents.

☛ 5. *Structured Confrontation.* The chemically dependent student is unlikely to respond successfully to any of these strategies and is in need of a professional assessment in the community, most likely followed by treatment. Her denial system, strong enough to resist these attempts to change her behavior, is likely to respond to the type of structured confrontation we are here considering for parents (see Chapter 8 and Appendix B).

A structured intervention with parents is often the vehicle for gaining parents' participation in steps 4 and 5.

PARENT TRIGGERS

What is the degree of parent denial?

The decision to intervene with parents is an increasingly realistic option, then, when the student has failed to change in response to school-based strategies. There are three other factors that must be considered in deciding to intervene with parents:

☞ Parents have previously demonstrated an unwillingness to become involved, or have exhibited some resistance to seeking appropriate help for their child.

☞ It seems unlikely that the family will **seek** professional help for their child–assessment or treatment–without the emotional and formal power of a structured confrontation. In other words, parent denial may be such that a casual recommendation for treatment or assessment by the counselor or principal will not be sufficient.

☞ It is unlikely that the family will **follow through** with professional recommendations without the power of a formal intervention. For example, "elopement"–leaving treatment programs prematurely–can be prevented if parents can be brought to see realistically the nature, scope, and implications of their child's condition.

SAP CORE TEAM PROCESS

Often it is possible for one person, usually a school counselor, to gain enough information about a student's condition and an accurate enough sense of the family's resistance to decide that intervening with parents is necessary. For some students the progression to chemical dependency or serious drug abuse is rapid, taking as little as a few months once drug use begins. The avalanche of harmful consequences at school, at home, and in the student's daily life, is equally swift.

In other circumstances the progression is more gradual and the decision to intervene with parents occurs within the context of a student assistance program utilizing a Core Team process. A Core Team, made up of administrators, counselors, support group leaders, and other interested staff, that manages a student's progress through the steps outlined above.*

Once a student comes to the attention of the Core Team, through staff referral, self-referral, policy violations, etc., the team begins the process of collecting preliminary data. This preliminary data comes from student

---

A full description of student assistance programs is beyond the scope of this discussion. See Anderson (1988) *When Chemicals Come to School: The Student Assistance Program Model.* Community Recovery Press, PO Box 20979, Greenfield, WI 53220.

records, teachers' reports, interviews with the student, and/or contacts with parents, peers, or siblings.

Smple Core Team meeting agenda This preliminary data is placed before the Core Team, which meets to answer the following questions:

1. How was the student referred?

2. What are the student's strengths?

3. What do we know (i.e., what data do we have)?

4. What questions do we have, or what do we need to know?

5. What action do we recommend, based on the *data we have* and the *data we need?* Typical courses of action include, in order of increasing seriousness:
    a. No apparent personal or performance problem at this time; no further action is necessary.
    b. No apparent alcohol/drug-related problem at this time; however, referral to other in-school or community services is appropriate for another problem.
    c. Further assessment interviews with the SAP counselor are needed.
    d. The student needs to contract for abstinence, monitored by frequent meetings between the student and the SAP counselor.
    e. The student needs to complete an in-school support group, after which additional recommendations may be made.
    f. The student requires an in-school assessment, involving the student, parents, and a certified alcohol/drug abuse counselor from an approved alcohol/drug agency.
    g. The student needs to have a formal assessment at a certified alcohol/drug agency, and to follow its recommendations.
    h. Pre-assessment evidence of chemical dependency supports the need for referral to a chemical dependency treatment program.

6. How will this recommendation be presented to the student?

7. How will we know it succeeded?

8. Who will follow-up, and when?

Involving parents as early as possible in this process is always wise. It becomes necessary at steps (f)-(h). When recommendations involving professional assessment or treatment are involved, a structured intervention with parents is often the recommendation of the Core Team under item 6.

ROLE OF THE FACILITATOR

Whether the decision to intervene with parents is made by a Core Team or by an individual, it will fall to an individual to begin orchestrating the intervention process. In the discussion which follows, the term **facilitator** will be used to refer to this individual. The facilitator's role consists of convening the intervention team and walking its members through the remaining tasks in preparation for the intervention meeting. While it will be assumed that the facilitator is a member of the school staff–most likely a counselor or another member of the pupil services staff–it can also be a drug abuse professional from a community alcohol/drug agency.

Since preparation is crucial, the facilitator's role is best fulfilled by someone who best meets several criteria:

> ★ The facilitator must have *access to as much preliminary data as possible* concerning the student's behaviors of concern, the steps the school has already taken, and the role parents have assumed thus far;

> ★ The facilitator should have *considerable training in alcohol and other drug abuse*, including the dynamics of drug abuse and dependency in adolescents and families, the nature of denial and enabling, the intervention process, and the assessment and treatment services available in the community;

> ★ The facilitator should have a *clear understanding of the intervention preparation process*;

> ★ The facilitator should have *the time necessary* to schedule and facilitate intervention team meetings (see Appendix C).

The person facilitating the preparation process is not necessarily the person who **moderates**, or chairs, the actual intervention meeting. The selection and role of this person will be described in Chapter 11, "Planning the Agenda."

CHAPTER FIVE

IDENTIFYING THE INTERVENTION TEAM

*If you confront alcoholism alone
you are outnumbered.*

A successful structured confrontation is conducted by a group of concerned individuals, or an intervention team. The need for a team is dictated solely by the nature of the denial system that results from alcohol and other drug abuse and dependency. The makeup of the intervention is also determined by the individual student and his family: the intervention team is composed of those who have a special relationship to both. Theoretically, the intervention team could be made up of different individuals for each student and family. The intervention facilitator, therefore, needs to understand the need for an intervention team, how to select team members, and how to involve them in the remaining steps of the intervention preparation process.

WHY A TEAM?

The quotation at the head of this chapter is an aphorism familiar to chemical dependency counselors. It reminds us that when we intervene we are confronting the denial system and not the person. It also reminds us of how complex alcohol and other drug abuse issues are. In confronting a chemically dependent individual, for example, we are up against his well-developed and practiced system of defenses, his need to protect his relationship with the drug, the message of enabling–by the significant people in his environment–that there is nothing wrong, and the other "absences" of information that contribute to his denial system. No one individual is likely to be successful against all of this. We can make a similar case against confronting parents alone.

No one individual has all the data

There are a number of specific reasons why an intervention team presents the best chance for success. First, no one individual has all the data concerning a student's behavior, or a complete picture of what is happening in his life. The adolescent who is seriously drug-involved becomes adept at isolating significant people in his environment from each other: school staff frequently do not talk to each other about behavior or report problems; family members do not talk about what is happening, or protect the adolescent from the consequences of his behavior; peers frequently have information that they do not share with each other; key segments of the community also interact with the student and see only a "slice" of the whole picture. Moreover, these various subsystems often do not communicate effectively with each other. No one, thus, sees the whole student or sees the pattern formed by individual episodes of behavior. A team, on the other hand, assembled from representatives of all of these segments of the student's environment, is much more likely to see accurately the nature, scope, and implications of the problem (see Chapter 7). Even if one individual had access to all of this information, and confronted parents with it, the data could be easily deflected or denied because it can appear to them to be second-hand, hearsay, or rumor. Or, parents can easily conclude that the confrontation is the idea of just one person. On the other hand, nothing has more emotional power than a group of significant, concerned individuals representing key segments of the student's world.

> *If one man tells you are a horse, he is probably a fool. If ten people tell you you are a horse, it's time to go out and buy a saddle.*

A team presents a unified goal

Secondly, a team is effective at reducing parent denial because it represents concerned individuals united by the same goal. An aspect of the family's response to drug abuse or dependency is its active struggle to change or cope with the student's behavior. Parents have typically tried many things to change their adolescent: arguing, cajoling, threatening, easing up on expectations, increasing expectations, giving privileges, taking away privileges, having more rules, having fewer rules, having more rules again, watching the student constantly, ignoring the behavior, hoping it will change by itself, etc. Parents will also have gotten advice from other family members and friends or from books, talk shows, and a host of other sources. A goal that seeks an assessment or treatment for a drug problem, presented by one individual, will be seen as just one in a long chain of remedies that have failed. Again, it is much more likely that the parents will listen seriously to a singular goal, legitimized by the data, and presented by a team that unanimously supports it (see Chapter 7).

A team presents a constellation of consequences

Third, consequences play a role in the intervention process. If parents resist the team's recommendations, each team member will share the natural, logical consequences for the student's failure to bring his behavior up to acceptable levels, or for the family's failure to support appropriate help. Because each member of the team has first-hand experience with the

> **An intervention team:**
>
> ❏ **Provides parents with a more complete and compelling picture of their child's problem;**
> ❏ **Presents a goal which many significant people agree is appropriate;**
> ❏ **Presents a group of consequences for the failure to change**
> ❏ **Presents a quantity of care and concern that reduces parent fears**

student's behavior, each has some specific way of reducing his or her enabling, or of allowing a consequence to be experienced. The consequences expressed by a team are more impactful than a single consequence (e.g., suspension) expressed by a single individual.

A team offers support

Finally, the emotional power of a team cannot be underestimated. Their denial will lead many parents to view the school as punitive or threatening, and to experience the intervention as something they need to protect themselves against. The manner of confrontation–sincere care and concern–manifested by the team and its members is a significant factor in helping parents to appreciate how many people in their child's life are worried and willing to help. In addition to its data, the team offers its support: the parents are not alone.

SELECTING TEAM MEMBERS

The team consists of "meaningful people"

Intervention team members are not selected according to their role in the school: i.e., because they are a principal or counselor. Team members are selected based (1) on the data they have concerning the student's behavior and (2) on their relevance to the student or parent. Intervention team members will be "meaningful" to either the student, the parents, or both. A "meaningful person" for intervention purposes will meet four criteria:

- ☛ He will have first-hand data or experience with the student's behavior;
- ☛ He will have some degree of care and concern for or emotional connection with the student or the parents;
- ☛ He will be willing to get more involved;
- ☛ He will have appropriate consequences that he is willing and able to carry out

In principle, *anyone* can be a member of the intervention team to the extent that he satisfies at least the first three of these criteria. Ideally, team members will represent a microcosm of the student's environment: school staff, family members, peers, and representatives of the wider community beyond school and family. There is a message in this constellation: the problem is not just the student, or home, or school. The problem and the concern about it reaches into every significant area of the student's life.

The facilitator of the intervention preparation should attempt to identify potential team members from each of these areas. Below are some suggestions for identifying intervention team members. In deciding who to involve, the facilitator should ask himself (1) who has first-hand data, (2) who has some degree of care and concern, (3) who would be willing to get involved, and (4) who has consequences he will enforce if the student fails to change or if the parents fail to support the offer of help?

School Staff

☑ *Teachers.* The student's teachers will often have excellent first-hand data on academic performance, classroom conduct, appearance, and attitude. A teacher whom the student respects or likes can be very effective, as well as the teacher who has had a good rapport with parents.

☑ *Administrators.* The administrator responsible for discipline (principal, assistant principal, dean) is almost always a member of the intervention team. The administrator probably has first-hand information about the student's conduct and is the only person who can enforce school policies by explaining the consequences to the student and/or parents for the student's failure to change.

☑ *Pupil Services Staff.* The guidance counselor, school social worker, school psychologist, school nurse, etc., may also have good, concrete information about the student. Counselors may also have interviewed the student, especially as part of the student assistance program process, and may have specific information concerning the student's alcohol or other drug abuse. The school nurse may have information about frequent visits to the health office, chronic health problems or suspected intoxication and "hangovers."

☑ *Coaches, Club/Activity Advisors.* Whether they currently participate or not, students who were once members of school organizations may have a enjoyed a special relationship with club advisors.

☑ *School Secretary/Attendance Clerk.* Attendance and tardiness data, often kept by office staff, can be shared by the school secretary or attendance clerk.

☑ *Support Group Leaders.* If a student has been a member of a support group related to the student assistance program, group leaders will likely have excellent information regarding the students's alcohol and other drug abuse, violations of abstinence contracts, failures to control chemical use, etc.

☑ *Bus Driver, Librarian, Custodian, Dietary Staff, etc.* Many individuals who interact with students may have witnessed behaviors that they have not formally reported, sometimes including critical incidents.

Family Members

☑ Family members undoubtedly have witnessed events first-hand which can make them important intervention team members. *Siblings* are often witnesses to episodes of drug abuse—e.g., coming home late, and misbehavior around the home—which they have not reported to parents. The same may be true for *extended family members* and *non-custodial parents.*

Peers

The facilitator should not be reluctant to reach out to various members of the student's social network in and outside of school. Students spend more time with each other than with adults, and peers have witnessed a lot of behavior which they have kept secret.

☑ *Current Friends.* While they may be reluctant to "narc" on a peer, some students will participate in an intervention process after they understand that it is designed to help rather than to punish.

☑ *Former Friends.* Many students will change peer groups as their alcohol and other drug abuse worsens. Old friends are abandoned because they will not tolerate the increased level of drug abuse, because drug abuse has harmed them somehow, or because a new peer group allows opportunities for drug abuse. Many former friends can also contribute their concern over the loss of the friendship due to chemicals.

☑ *Team-mates, Club Members.* As their drug abuse worsens, many students who were once involved in athletics or other extracurricular activities will drop out of them. Their former teammates often have good data concerning the change in their behavior or performance.

Community

A student's behavior may be visible to segments of the wider community. Representatives from these areas can be key members of the intervention team, as their data communicates to parents the broadness of the concern and, in some cases, the seriousness of the consequences if problem behavior continues.

☑ *Law Enforcement.* The troubled student may have had contact with several areas of law enforcement or the juvenile justice system. *Police officers* may have data about contacts they have had with a student which did not result in an arrest or other formal action. *Probation/parole officers* may be able to make assessment and treatment a condition for probation. They can sometimes give parents a clear picture of the consequences for the next illegal act. Other *juvenile justice workers,* attached to juvenile courts, can make a reduction in sentencing conditional upon successful treatment for chemical dependency.

☑ *Others.* The *employers* of those students with jobs are often able to contribute information concerning unacceptable job performance. *Clergy,* if they don't have specific information about the student, can be supportive of the parents' decision to seek help. *Neighbors or parents' friends* often have data to contribute. They can often remind parents of what they have seen or talked to them about, or of how long the problem has been continuing. The *parents of the student's friends* may also have important data to contribute.

In short, the student who is in serious trouble will have encountered many people in various areas of his life who will have some degree of first-hand data to contribute to the intervention process. Few students or families are so isolated that no "meaningful people" can be found.

ASSEMBLING THE TEAM

The difficulty we sometimes experience in intervening with students or parents thus does not stem from the absence of significant people. It is most often due to the difficulty of identifying them and convening these meaningful persons. One of the important tasks of the intervention facilitator, then, is to identify these meaningful persons before contacting them personally to ask them if they would be willing to participate in an intervention. The *preliminary* intervention team consists of everyone who can be identified and is willing to be involved. Not everyone who joins this preliminary team may take part in the structured confrontation. As the remainder of the preparation process unfolds, individuals may drop out. It is also conceivable that a preliminary team of 20 people could be assembled, whereas only seven or eight might be necessary for the confrontation with parents. The facilitator, with the group's input, would select those who would participate in the actual intervention. These decisions are typically made just prior to planning the meeting's agenda (see Chapter 11 and Appendix C).

The preliminary versus the actual intervention team

The remaining steps in assembling the preliminary intervention team include the following:

1. **Contact** the potential participant personally.

2. **Explain your concern**. Summarize the information you have already that legitimizes your concern for the student, being careful not to disclose confidential information (see "Legal Issues" in Appendix A).

3. **Explain that you want to meet with parents** to communicate your concern, and you are contacting other meaningful people for their help.

4. **Tell the potential team members that you suspect they may have good data** about the student's behavior, or that they have a special relationship with the student or parents, or that they may have effective consequences.

5. **Explain the process briefly**. The team will have to spend a few meetings in preparation for a confrontation with parents.

Dealing with participants' objections

6. **Ask** if they would be willing to participate. Not all of those who *could* participate *will.* The facilitator should be prepared to address the objections or resistance that some may have. It is useful to meet with the reluctant team member to discuss his concerns before meeting as a team. Some may resist the idea of confrontation itself due to misunderstandings they have about it: that it is angry, hostile, or punitive. The facilitator needs to explain that the meeting will be guided by care and concern. Other potential participants may fear risking the relationship they have with either the student or the parents. Some discussion of the seriousness of the student's condition or of enabling issues may be helpful, especially with a student's peers, siblings, or others close to him or his family. Still others may have experienced failure in working with the student or the parents in the past. The facilitator can explain that a formal, structured intervention is very successful and has not yet been tried.

Having identified and contacted the significant people in the student and his family's environment, the facilitator can assemble the preliminary intervention team for its first meeting.

WORKSHEET 5.1

The worksheet on the next page can help the facilitator in assembling a preliminary intervention team. In addition to their role, name, and contact information (phone, etc.), there are places for estimating individuals' potential strengths (Might they have good data? Is it alcohol/drug specific ('AODA')?, etc.). The facilitator can also utilize the worksheet for keeping track of team members' attendance at subsequent meetings.

Worksheet 5.1
Preliminary Intervention Team Roster

Relationship to Student	Name	Contact Info	Good Data?	AODA?	Good Consequences?	Good Rel. to Student?	Good Rel. to Parents?	Willing?	Attended: Date	Date	Date	Date	Date
School Staff:													
Teacher													
Teacher													
Teacher													
Teacher													
Teacher													
Teacher													
Administrator													
Counselor													
Group Leader													
Social Worker													
Psychologist													
Nurse													
Coach													
Advisor													
Attendance Clerk													
Other:													
Other													
Other													
Peers:													
Current Friend													
Current Friend													
Former Friend													
Former Friend													
Teammates													
Others													
Family:													
Parent													
Sibling													
Sibling													
Other:													
Other:													
Community:													
Employer													
Police Officer													
Probation/Parole													
Juvenile Justice													
Clergy													
Other:													
Others:													

 **C**HAPTER **SIX**

EDUCATING THE TEAM

Role of the facilitator

One of the key tasks of the intervention facilitator is to educate the intervention team in two areas: information about the intervention process, and content issues involving alcohol and other drug abuse. Members of the assembled intervention team need a basic awareness of the intervention process in order to continue. They need to know what precipitated the decision to intervene with parents. They need to know what steps will have to be taken in order to prepare for the structured confrontation, what kind of time commitment will be required of them, and how many times the team will have to meet. They also will need to know something about the

Content and process

confrontation meeting itself. In addition, members should ideally share a basic understanding of some fundamental issues surrounding alcohol and other drug abuse and chemical dependency. It is important for team members to have a working familiarity, at least, with the distinction between drug use, abuse, and chemical dependency, with the nature of denial and enabling, and with family dynamics. They should also be aware of the school's existing alcohol and other drug abuse services for students, or with its student assistance program. The first meeting of the preliminary team is often devoted to addressing these areas.

CONTENT AREAS

The preparation tasks of the intervention team require its members to make number of decisions: e.g., evaluating the data it has and selecting appropriate details, recommending an appropriate goal to parents, determining appropriate consequences for the student's failure to change, developing consequences for the parents' failure to support assessment or treatment, and more. Where alcohol and other drug abuse are concerned, these decisions are not arbitrary but are informed by two major issues: (1) the nature of alcohol and other drug abuse and how it affects students and families, and (2) the history of working with the student and/or the parents within existing school programs and services.

Alcohol and Other Drug Abuse

Team members need to share an awareness of the seriousness of alcohol and other drug abuse by students, regardless of the kinds of drugs used, or of the frequency or amounts used. None of the major mood-alterers, especially alcohol, is "safer" than any other. Furthermore, while physical harm is always a concern, the actual or potential harm to normal psycho-social growth and development presents more lasting and subtle problems. Abstinence is the primary goal for students. It is important for team members to at least be familiar with, if not share, the basic philosophy of "zero tolerance" for kids. The issue for a student becomes, then, not what or how often they are abusing, but their inability or unwillingness to stop despite attempts to help them. A commitment to abstinence is fundamental to answering the question "Why do we need to do this?"

Chemical Dependency

The same arguments apply in favor of participants having some familiarity with the nature of chemical dependency. Though all team members do not need much information about its specific signs and symptoms, they do benefit from understanding that chemical dependency is a *primary, progressive, chronic, and ultimately fatal illness.* Understanding that chemical dependency is a primary, autonomous illness—which progresses, once contracted, independent of any pre-existing causes or conditions—prevents team members from avoiding the intervention in favor of other strategies ("Maybe if the student just got involved in extracurricular activities"). As a progressive illness, chemical dependency will always worsen without appropriate treatment (versus "It's a phase; they'll grow out of it"). Chronicity means "incurable." Abstinence, not "cutting down," is the only safe course for the chemically dependent adolescent. Finally, without appropriate treatment, chemical dependency results in a premature death, through overdose, accidents, suicide, violence, medical complications, poor nutrition, and so on. Understanding the fatal nature of the disease empowers people (including parents) to take difficult but necessary stances regarding the necessity for treatment and abstinence.

Denial and Enabling

Potential intervention participants need to understand that parents lack the information they need to agree to get their child help, and that their outward behavior, no matter how unpleasant, is self-protective and not mean-spirited. They also need to know that the purpose of intervention is to confront this denial system, not the parents. The more team members understand about the nature of denial, the more likely they are to appreciate the emotional dynamics of the intervention process. An intervention does not succeed because we have better arguments or clearer logic than parents.

The team member also needs to be familiar with the concept of "enabling," and with how it applies both to parents' reactions to their child as well as to her own interactions with the student. Because the ideal team member has first-hand experience with the student's behavior, she may have been involved in some enabling herself. An understanding of enabling assists team members in determining appropriate consequences for the student's failure to change, or for the parents' unwillingness to support a referral for assessment or treatment.

Family Issues Finally, alcohol and other drug abuse and dependency affects families and other systems as well as individuals. Understanding the family's denial, its behavioral reactions to the student's erratic and dangerous behavior, and how its emotional pain is hidden by ego defenses can help team members to see the intervention as a "care and concern" meeting.

Educating About Content

Some combination of several strategies can give team members the necessary working knowledge of alcohol and other drug abuse. Hopefully, many participants will bring to the team some background in these areas through formal training or inservice. Schools with student assistance programs will have made "Core Training" available to administrators, pupil services staff members, support group leaders, and interested teachers and other staff. Periodic inservice of all staff members has often provided most school staff with some familiarity with these concepts. It is also a relatively simple matter to prepare a handout that summarizes these issues and to give it to prospective team members as they are recruited. In addition, the facilitator will have to do some explicit educating as part of the remaining preparation tasks. In summarizing the factors that precipitated the need to intervene, for example, the facilitator can briefly describe the nature of drug abuse or the evidence that leads the school to suspect chemical dependency (within the limits of confidentiality—see Appendix A), and so on. Finally, the questions of team members at each subsequent preparation stage will present opportunities for providing relevant background information.

Team members need to know that the process of preparing to intervene is in many ways more important than what happens during the confrontation itself.

PROCESS AREAS

Those intervention team members who are not school staff, who are not Core Team members within a student assistance program, or who have not participated in an intervention before, will need to know something about the process. Some will need to know what the process will be before they can agree to participate. In general, the intervention facilitator will need to give team members information about the process of intervening, about the number of meetings that will be required of them for preparation, about the specific preparations tasks that remain, and about their personal role in the parent confrontation. Team members will also need to know what circumstances have precipitated the need to intervene with parents.

Specifically, the following areas should be addressed:

❏ The school has developed a concern about a student's behavior and feels that help outside the school is required.

❏ The school feels that parents are unwilling or unable to respond to a casual request that they seek such help for their child and that the help of several significant individuals will be required.

❏ Since the welfare of the student is seriously in doubt, and ultimately at stake, the school wishes to prepare carefully to insure a successful outcome when parents are confronted with its concerns.

❏ You will need to get together as a team on four occasions before the meeting with parents to do the following:

1. Review your concerns, describe the preparation process, and prepare to collect relevant data for the intervention;

2. Pool and evaluate the data of team members

3. Decide on a recommendation to make to parents and define the consequences for the student's failure bring her conduct up to acceptable levels;

4. Prepare responses to parents' objections and/or resistance, and plan the intervention meeting.

Educating About Process

The facilitator can educate members about the intervention preparation process in two general ways. First, it is often wise, when they are first contacted and invited to participate, to give team members a memo or handout that describes the process along the lines above. Second, the first meeting with team members is often devoted to describing and setting the remaining agenda and preparing the team for collecting data. (Appendix C provides more detailed suggestions for the facilitator on the agenda for each preparation meeting).

Despite the discussion above, educating team members about what intervention is about need not be complicated or highly structured. Of all the preparation tasks it can be handled the most casually and can be based on the amount of time the facilitator has and on the needs of prospective intervention team members.

CHAPTER SEVEN

COLLECTING DATA

Many confrontations with parents have gone wrong because care was not taken in assembling appropriate data. Either it was too general, too narrow, or irrelevant to the confrontation. As indicated in Chapter 3, we are confronting denial, not parents. What we confront with are facts, or data. Aside from preparation, the quantity and quality of the data used in the intervention is perhaps the most important contributor to its success. To gauge its appropriateness and relevance the data must be carefully collected and reviewed in advance of the intervention meeting.

THE IMPORTANCE OF DATA

Legitimacy

The data with which parents are to be confronted is vital to the success of the intervention to the degree that it lends *legitimacy* to the intervention process, and to the extent that it addresses their *denial*.

Good data lends legitimacy to the entire intervention process. The factual information about a student's behavior is what legitimizes our concern (some refer to data as "behaviors of concern") and our decision to intervene in the first place. The data that individual team members bring to the confrontation also legitimizes *their participation* in the confrontation. Good data also lends legitimacy to the *goal* of the intervention. A request that their child seek an assessment and/or treatment for drug abuse, for example, will appear illegitimate to parents without factual information to support the request. Finally, if parents are informed of the consequences of their child's failure to change or of their failure to seek help, those consequences will easily appear punitive, controlling, or manipulative if they are not validated by sufficient behavioral data about the student.

Denial   Aside from lending credibility to the process, good data also functions to address the basic nature of the denial system: the absence of information that constitutes parents' inability to appreciate the nature, scope, and implications of their student's problem. Effective data will include those many episodes of unacceptable, violent or dangerous conduct that parents have rationalized away or forgotten. Because drug abuse and dependency tend to isolate the individual from others, effective data will also include other episodes of behavior that have been witnessed by others in the student's life but never shared with parents, giving them a more complete picture of the "whole person."

CHARACTERISTICS OF GOOD DATA

First-hand   The most useful facts illustrating a student's problems will be first-hand information. First-hand information consists of behaviors which the team member has actually seen, witnessed, or been involved with. First-hand data, expressed with "I" statements, will have the most cognitive and emotional impact for parents, and will invite the least resistance. Effective intervention data, therefore, must *not* consist of generalizations: "John has a negative attitude in class." While this may be true, team members must be encouraged to be specific. A teacher's perception of John's negative attitude must be based on a series of observed details: *"During the past three months, John does not respond in class and has not handed in any work. Last week I had to reprimand him for calling another student a 'slut.'"* Many schools with student assistance programs will help staff members to be specific by providing them with referral forms consisting of representative behaviors of concern (see Worksheet 7.1).

Detailed   Good data must not consist of rumors or opinions. Rumors, for example, like "Other teachers say his grades are falling;" or "All the kids say he gets drunk a lot", or opinions ("I think he gets high after school") will typically not be taken as facts by parents and will usually provoke a verbal denial. One way of avoiding rumors is to speak personally: *"John's grades are falling in my class, from a C to a D+."* Another is to have documentation: a counselor can report that John's grades last quarter have averaged a D+. Another way of avoiding rumors and opinions is to invite those other staff members or students to be participants in the intervention, where they can speak personally about what they have witnessed.

Sometimes effective data is not, strictly speaking, "first-hand." A probation officer may not have *witnessed* a student being arrested for driving under the influence. That the student was arrested is not, however, a rumor, generalization, or opinion and can be an effective piece of data.

SOURCES OF INTERVENTION DATA

Just as team members were selected in part because they represent key segments of the student's life, the data they collect and subsequently share with parents should ideally represent the student's behavior in these areas as well. Data from at least the following eight areas can insure a successful intervention with parents (examples of specific behaviors can be found in Worksheets 7.1 and 7.2):

❑ School Performance
❑ Family Problems
❑ Peer Relationships
❑ Law Enforcement
❑ Personality Changes
❑ Financial Problems
❑ Physical Health Problems
❑ Alcohol/Drug Specific Problems

ALCOHOL/DRUG–SPECIFIC DATA

Objective vs. personal data

Where alcohol and other drug abuse are a key concern, specific, AODA-related data must be gathered as well. A pattern of behavioral problems is grounds for referring a family to help; it is necessary, however, to establish a pattern of alcohol/drug-specific behavior if a specific form of help (assessment or treatment) is to be recommended. Though what has been said about data above applies to all types, alcohol/drug-specific data presents some unique issues of its own. The nature of the data and how it is presented depends on whether it is *objective* or *personal*. By *objective* alcohol and other drug abuse data is meant that information which is a matter of record (formal or informal) with school staff, law enforcement, or others. *Personal* data, on the other hand, consists of the experiences witnessed by affected others–those who have been personally affected and/or who have experienced some degree of emotional pain because of the student's alcohol/drug abuse. There are different guidelines for each.

Objective Data

School staff are likely to have alcohol and other drug-specific facts which they can contribute to the intervention if care is taken to observe restrictions imposed by confidentiality (see Appendix A, "Legal Issues"). A counselor, as part of the Core Team process in a student assistance program, would have interviewed the student following his referral, asking questions about his experience with alcohol or other drugs. Support group leaders are also likely to have information concerning the student's drug abuse, including his attempts to control it, violations of the support group's abstinence contract, etc. Disciplinary actions taken on the basis of the student's violations of school policies against possession, use delivery, or sale in school are also vital. In some cases, such violations are important precipitating events for the intervention process.

Alcohol/drug abuse   Parents need some indication of the degree of their student's alcohol/drug involvement. Any information along the following lines is useful:

❏ The *kinds* and *number* of substances abused (e.g., alcohol, marijuana, cocaine, etc.)
❏ The *frequency* of use (daily, weekly, weekends, etc.)
❏ The *amounts* of use (e.g., the numbers of drinks on a typical occasion)
❏ The *age* at which use began
❏ The *consequences* of use (e.g., "John was caught drinking in school and was suspended," or "John said that he has been partying so much on weekends that he can't get to school on Mondays").

Information about alcohol and other drug abuse should be reported accurately. There is a difference between "Your son is using alcohol every day" and "Your son reported in the support group that he drank every day."

Chemical dependency   On some occasions the school will have grounds to suspect chemical dependency. While the school, as a rule, cannot diagnose the illness, it can collect sufficient information to suspect it. The suspicion that a student might be chemically dependent often develops after all the data concerning a student is pooled and reviewed by the intervention team. Counselors, support group leaders, or others who worked closely with the student should be alert for signs of the following indicators of chemical dependency:*

❏ *Loss of control,* or the inability to predict the consequences once an episode of drug abuse begins (e.g., unsuccessful attempts to quit, unsuccessful attempts to control; breaking abstinence contracts; continued abuse despite the experience of harmful consequences)
❏ *Harmful consequences,* or a pattern of harmful consequences that occur as a direct result of drug abuse
❏ *"Characterological conflict,"* or behavior, caused by drug abuse, that violates the student's own values, goals, aspirations
❏ *Drug-related low self-worth:* low self-esteem caused by doing things while intoxicated that violate the student's values
❏ *Drug-centered life-style,* or *preoccupation:* devoting a considerable amount of mental, emotional, and social energy to the drug relationship
❏ *Tolerance,* or the tendency to increase the dose over time, because the body needs a larger dose to achieve the same effect.
❏ *Blackouts,* or the inability to recall later what happens while intoxicated

---

* For a more complete discussion of chemical dependency and its assessment, see (Anderson (1988), pp. 139-153; Johnson (1980); and McAuliffe and McAuliffe (1975a and 1975b).

Personal Data

There are many individuals for whom knowledge of the student's drug abuse is not objective but is more personal and close to home. These individuals have not only witnessed the drug abuse but have been personally affected by it emotionally. These members of the intervention team will most often be peers, boyfriends or girlfriends, siblings, and sometimes a parent or other relative. Personal data should be collected as narrative episodes, rather than as factual information.

Characteristics of effective personal data

Experience proves that, to be effective, an episode of personal data should have six characteristics:

1. **The personal data should concern an incident when the student's drug abuse caused a specific problem or harm**. There may be many problems in a student's relationships, for example. The only ones relevant for intervening will be those caused by drug abuse.

2. **The personal data must be first-hand**, consisting of events which the team member has witnessed himself.

3. **The personal data should be developed with significant details**, yet it should be brief. The most useful details include the occasion (*"On our date last weekend..."*), the specific drug abuse behavior (*"John smoked so much marijuana..."*), the harmful outcome (*"that he couldn't drive, and when I said I wanted to he kicked me out of the car and said we were breaking up."*), how the intervenor was affected emotionally at the time (*"I felt scared, hurt, and angry."*) and how she may have enabled at the time (*"I didn't tell you or anybody because I didn't want to get him in trouble"*).

4. **The event should make a clear and definite connection between drug abuse and the harmful consequences that resulted.** Parents may think that their student abuses drugs because he has problems; they need to see that the reverse is true.

5. **The data should include how the intervenor was affected emotionally**. Painful feelings are the least visible or talked about of the consequences of drug abuse.

6. **The data should indicate how the intervenor may have enabled at the time,** by protecting, not talking, helping the student out of trouble, etc. Parents need to see that they have not witnessed and their child has not experienced all of the consequences of his drug abuse.

Worksheet 7.3 can be a useful tool for helping team members to generate and organize personal alcohol/drug data.

Facilitator's role   Data gathered from a variety of sources, reflecting general behaviors of concern as well as objective and personal data about drug abuse will send a powerful message of legitimacy to parents during the intervention meeting, providing them with a much deeper appreciation of the nature, scope, and implications of their child's problem. The facilitator plays a crucial role in this preparation step by insuring that the data is appropriate, relevant, and specific. He will educate team members as to what kinds of data will be appropriate before they meet to pool it. As individual team members share their data with the team, the facilitator will also be evaluating it and helping them to modify it in the most impactful direction (see Appendix C).

WORKSHEET 7.1

Worksheet 7.1, "Sample SAP Referral Form," is an example of a list of "behaviors of concern" that can be given to teachers and other school staff. Though it was developed originally as a referral form for student assistance programs it can also help intervention team members to document objective data for intervention.

WORKSHEET 7.2

Worksheet 7.2, "Signs of Possible Alcohol/Drug Abuse–For Family Members" is a lengthy list of behavioral signs that may be associated with adolescent drug abuse that has progressed to serious stages. Occasionally, a parent or other family member will be a member of the intervention team. The checklist can assist them in recalling behaviors they have seen but forgotten and which may indicate a serious problem.

WORKSHEET 7.3

Worksheet 7.3, "Personal Data Sheet–Alcohol/Drug-Specific," helps team members who have personal experiences with a student's alcohol/drug abuse to organize their data and to be selective about the relevant details.

Worksheet 7.1
Sample SAP Referral Form

Referral of troubled students to the student assistance program must be based upon observed behaviors. As a rule, an isolated instance of poor or unsatisfactory performance will not be grounds for a referral. However, whenever a student exhibits several of the following, or when there is a definite and repeated pattern of behavior in an unacceptable direction, a referral to the SAP staff is appropriate. Please give this completed form to the SAP Coordinator at your school.

Student: _____ Grade: ___ Referral date: _____ Referred by: _____

I. Academic Performance
____ Decline in quality of work
____ Decline in grade earned
____ Incomplete work
____ Work not handed in
____ Failing in this subject
Comments: _____
_____
_____
_____
_____
_____
_____

II. Classroom Conduct
____ Disruptive in class
____ Inattentive
____ Lack of concentration
____ Lack of motivation
____ Sleeping in class
____ Impaired memory
____ Negative attitude
____ In-school absenteeism (skipping)
____ Tardiness to class
____ Disturbs others
____ Defiance; breaking rules
____ Frequently needs discipline
____ Cheating
____ Fighting
____ Throwing objects
____ Defiance of authority
____ Verbally abusive
____ Obscene language, gestures
____ Sudden outbursts of temper
____ Vandalism
____ Frequent visits to nurse
____ Frequent visits to lavatory
____ Nervousness, anxiety
____ Comments: _____
_____
_____
_____

III. Other Behavior
____ Erratic behavior day-to-day
____ Change in friends and/or peer group
____ Sudden, unexplained popularity
____ Mood swings
____ Seeks constant adult contact
____ Seeks adult advice without a specific problem
____ Time disorientation
____ Apparent changes in personal values
____ Depression
____ Low affect
____ Defensiveness
____ Withdrawal; a loner; separateness from others
____ Other student express concerns about
____ Fantasizing, daydreaming
____ Compulsive achievement
____ Preoccupation with school success
____ Perfectionism
____ Difficulty in accepting mistakes
____ Rigid obedience
____ Talks freely about drug use; bragging
____ Associates with known drug users
____ Comments:
_____
_____
_____
_____
_____

IV. Possible Alcohol/Drug-Specific Behaviors

Witnessed	Suspected	
_____	_____	Selling; delivering
_____	_____	Possession of alcohol/drugs
_____	_____	Possession of paraphernalia
_____	_____	Use of alcohol or other drugs
_____	_____	Intoxication
_____	_____	Physical signs, symptoms
_____	_____	Others?

Use the back of this form to comment specifically on each behavior checked.

Worksheet 7.2
Signs of Possible Alcohol/Drug Abuse
For Family Members

Adolescence can be a troubling, confusing time for both young people and their family members. In becoming alert to the possibility of an alcohol/drug problem, it is necessary to attempt to separate those adolescent behaviors which are transitory indications of the struggle to "grow up" from those which often indicate the presence of alcohol/drug abuse.

The following are offered as signs which may alert parents to potentially serious alcohol/drug involvement.

DECLINE IN SCHOOL PERFORMANCE:

COMMENTS:

- ❏ An atypical decline in grades during the past year;
- ❏ A rapid, recent decline in grades
- ❏ Failure to inform parents of school events, including requests for parents to meet with teachers, suspensions, etc.
- ❏ Loss of interest in school activities, including dropping out of athletics, clubs, or other extracurricular activities
- ❏ Contacts from the school regarding truancy, tardiness, dropping classes, vandalism, fighting, thefts, or other unacceptable conduct

PROBLEMS WITH LAW ENFORCEMENT:

- ❏ Arrests for driving under the influence (DUI)
- ❏ Arrests for drinking/drug use at parties or in public places
- ❏ Arrests for possession, delivery, or sale of alcohol or other drugs
- ❏ Curfew violations
- ❏ Other illegal acts which only occur when he/she is under the influence of alcohol or other drugs

PROBLEMS WITH FINANCES:

- ❏ Involved in thefts
- ❏ Family members begin missing money or valuables from the home
- ❏ Frequent borrowing of money from family members or friends
- ❏ Quitting a job and/or job loss due to unsatisfactory job performance
- ❏ Inability to save money or to pay bills despite having a job or allowance
- ❏ Sale of clothes, records, stereos, or other possessions
- ❏ Appears to have sufficient spending money despite not having a job
- ❏ Appears to have more spending money than allowance or job would provide
- ❏ Is often seen exchanging money with friends

PEER RELATIONSHIPS:

❏ Appears to have changed to a set of friends who are increas-ingly objectionable; "reputation" suffers
❏ Sudden popularity with a peer group that is significantly younger or older
❏ Rarely brings new friends home to meet family members
❏ Old friends are rejected or are no longer seen by family
❏ Change to a group of friends where chemical use seems to be more frequent or acceptable (i.e., new friends talk frequently about 'getting high,' 'partying,' etc., or wear jewelry or clothing with drug-related themes)
❏ Former friends, their parents, and/or neighbors express concern

PERSONALITY CHANGES, EMOTIONAL PROBLEMS:

❏ Frequent, extreme highs and lows
❏ General change in mood toward a more depressed and negative or critical outlook
❏ Withdrawal from family members
❏ Is more secretive; stays physically isolated in room, withdraws into music
❏ Increasing dishonesty; frequent lying; elaborate stories or excuses
❏ Is increasingly defensive when asked about personal problems, when confronted with irresponsibility, etc.
❏ Avoids communication with family members; spends a lot of time alone
❏ Is increasingly angry, defiant
❏ Is verbally and/or physically abusive
❏ Exhibits general loss of energy, initiative, motivation, interest, or enthusiasm; is increasingly apathetic
❏ Daily routine becomes inverted: frequently stays out late and sleeps late in the morning
❏ General psychological impairment: inability to reason; memory loss; inability to think logically; feelings of paranoia

PHYSICAL PROBLEMS:

❏ Appears run-down; has frequent colds, flu, or other illnesses due to decreased immunity
❏ Loss of normal appetite
❏ Decline in personal hygiene; bathes infrequently, doesn't change clothes, etc.
❏ Drastic weight gain or loss
❏ Complexion appears unhealthy: is sometimes pale or flushed, has bloodshot eyes, face looks puffy
❏ Has frequent injuries or bruises which may or may not have a satisfactory explanation (e.g., 'I just fell down')
❏ Has self-inflicted tatoos, cigarette burns, scars
❏ Suffers from insomnia or other sleep disturbances; or, chronic fatigue, tiredness;
❏ Chronic dry cough
❏ Changes in menstrual cycle

ALCOHOL/DRUG-SPECIFIC INDICATORS:

COMMENTS:

- ❏ Adolescent vehemently asserts his/her right to drink or to get high
- ❏ Smell of alcohol on the breath, or of marijuana on clothing
- ❏ Bloodshot eyes, dilated or constricted pupils
- ❏ Blackouts: inability to remember events which occur while out or while intoxicated
- ❏ Presence of drug paraphernalia: roach clips, "bongs," cellophane bags, drug-related posters, cocaine spoons, crack vials, cigarette papers, pipes, bottles, etc.
- ❏ Discovery of unidentified pills or powders; discovery of alcohol, drugs, or paraphernalia among personal effects, especially when effort has gone into hiding them
- ❏ Smell of incense in room or on clothing (to hide odor of marijuana)
- ❏ Clothing with drug-related themes; drug-related drawings on books, clothing, or body
- ❏ Returning home intoxicated; staggering, slurred speech, incoherence
- ❏ Talks freely about getting high and uses a vocabulary typical among regular drug users
- ❏ Family liquor supply dwindles, disappears, or gets watered-down
- ❏ Medications begin disappearing from family medicine cabinet

DISRUPTION OF FAMILY RELATIONSHIPS:

- ❏ Increasing irresponsibility in the family; fails to do chores, carry out normal tasks
- ❏ Defies family rules without regard to consequences
- ❏ Avoids or decreases participation in family social gatherings and rituals, such as holiday gatherings, vacations, meals, church activities, etc.
- ❏ Increasingly feels like a stranger to the rest of the family
- ❏ Behavior incites or aggravates increasing tension between parents
- ❏ Is verbally or physically abusive to parents or siblings
- ❏ Family members become more fearful of the adolescent
- ❏ Stays out late or does not return home at all despite increasingly stringent consequences
- ❏ Blames problems on parents and/or other family members;
- ❏ Avoids contact with family members; goes immediately to room when returning home; is secretive about friends, phone calls, activities, or whereabouts
- ❏ Family members become increasingly preoccupied with the adolescent as the center of their anger, apprehension, and suspicion, or of their care and concern

(Adapted from Anderson, *(1988) When Chemicals Come to School, pp. 132-135.* Used by permission).

Worksheet 7.3
Personal Data Sheet (Alcohol/Drug-Specific)

What was the occasion (date, place)?	What was the specific drug-using behavior? (E.g., drinking, drug use)	What was the harmful outcome (what happened)?	What was your emotional reaction? (E.g., "I felt....")	What did you do at the time that might have been 'enabling?'
"On our date last weekend..."	John smoked so much marijuana that he couldn't drive. When I asked to drive	"...he kicked me out of the car and said he was breaking up with me."	"I felt angry, afraid, and hurt."	"I didn't tell anyone because I didn't want to get him in trouble."

C HAPTER EIGHT

DECIDING ON A GOAL

By collecting and pooling its data, the intervention team has done an informal "pre-assessment." For our purposes, the term "assessment" does not mean "diagnosis." To assess means to gather information about the student's behavior and to interpret that information based on what the team knows about drug abuse and dependency. The data collection step provides the team with a comprehensive idea of the nature, scope, and implications of the student's problem. Armed with this picture, the team next must decide (1) what it wants the student to do, and (2) what it wants the parents to do. The decision it makes in these two areas constitutes the goal of the intervention meeting.

TYPES OF GOALS

As we have stressed, the general goal is for a student to maintain continuous abstinence from the use of alcohol or other drugs. The specific goal of the intervention concerns how best this can be accomplished, determined by the data collected. There exist a variety of possible goals, depending on the nature and severity of the student's alcohol and other drug abuse.

Chemical Dependency

Primary Treatment

The data collected by school staff, the student's failure to change despite the school's previous attempts at help, and the parents' past refusal to become involved may all be evidence of chemical dependency. Whenever chemical dependency is suspected, the optimal goal is primary treatment for the illness through a community agency on either an inpatient or outpatient basis.

Liability for cost

Direct referral to chemical dependency treatment remains problematic and may not be wise. The potential financial liability for the school is the major argument against having the intervention team recommend chemical dependency treatment as its goal. If the school directly refers the student and/or her family to a specific treatment program, many have argued that the school my be held liable for the cost of treatment. (Reports of the cost for a one-month stay in a residential chemical dependency treatment center range from $9,000 to $60,000 or more—or from $300 to $2,000 per day). Avoiding referral to a specific program by presenting parents with a choice between several treatment programs does not guarantee that the school cannot be held liable for treatment costs. Until legal issues at the state and federal level are clarified involving chemical dependency as an illness and a handicapping condition, schools should avoid direct referral to treatment as their primary intervention goal.

Professional AODA assessment

Treatment for chemical dependency is by no means the only intervention goal. Where chemical dependency is suspected, one of the most appropriate goals is for parents *to agree to obtain a professional assessment* for chemical dependency though a community alcohol/drug abuse agency, and t*o agree to follow the agency's recommendations*. A screening or assessment can be obtained through treatment hospitals or other residential programs, through agencies which specialize in alcohol/drug assessments, or through private therapists. It is necessary that the screening be alcohol/drug-specific. Both assessment programs and private therapists should be evaluated by the school before they are included on the list of suggested services for parents (see Worksheet 8.1).

Working relationships with assessment agencies

In suggesting a professional assessment to parents it is also important for the school to have established good working relationships with those agencies or professionals it will recommend. Parents will have questions about the process, who to contact, cost, and what will happen during the assessment. Someone on the intervention team will have to be prepared to answer these questions and concerns accurately (see Chapter 9, also).

It is also a good idea to offer parents a choice between several assessment programs which the school believes are trustworthy. The cost of assessments is usually small. Publicly funded programs typically utilize a sliding scale, based on the family's ability to pay, and insurance should cover all or part of the cost. In addition, many agencies will provide free assessments. For these reasons, the question of the school's potential liability for the cost of assessment has not been as problematic as the same issues surrounding treatment.

In deciding on assessment as its goal, the intervention team should be wary of programs that conduct only brief "one-shot" interviews with students or parents. There is wide agreement that the assessment of chemical dependency in adolescents is difficult at best. The assessment should be a process, involving several interviews. The input of the school's intervention team is vital, as it provides the assessment program with information against which it can judge the responses of the student and her parents during the evaluation process.

Release of information forms

Providing this information to the assessing program requires the school to execute a "General Consent for the Release of Information Form." The release of information form is required by federal confidentiality regulations (see Appendix A). If parents agree with this goal, the school will want to obtain feedback from the assessment agency concerning the results of the assessment and the degree of the student and her family's compliance with its recommendations. Alcohol/drug agencies are also required by statute to have a release of information, signed by the student and/or her parents, before such information can be released to the school. The school can obtain in advance two releases of information—one permitting the school's disclosures to the agency and one permitting the agency's disclosures to the school (see Worksheet 8.2).

Alcohol and Other Drug Abuse

Ironically, the intervention goal for the student who is not chemically dependent can be more complex. The general goal is still abstinence. Deciding on the vehicle by which to achieve it often involves a choice between (1) an assessment, as above, (2) abstinence supported by community-based services, (3) abstinence supported by in-school services, (4) behavioral contracting, or (5) a combination of several of the above.

Assessment

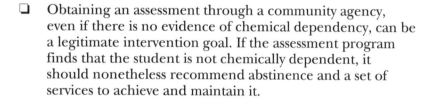 Obtaining an assessment through a community agency, even if there is no evidence of chemical dependency, can be a legitimate intervention goal. If the assessment program finds that the student is not chemically dependent, it should nonetheless recommend abstinence and a set of services to achieve and maintain it.

Community-based services

❏ The intervention team may select as its goal that the parent enroll the student in various community services aimed at helping adolescents to stay drug-free. Many agencies offer programs combining education, counseling, and support for both the student and her family.

School-based services

❏ If the school has a student assistance program it probably offers a number of services for students who are abusing alcohol or other drugs. One of the more common is the use-focussed support group. This group is designed for students who are actively involved in drug abuse. Its primary goal is to help students achieve abstinence by providing them with the personal insight and skills necessary to do so (see Anderson (1988), pp. 311-326). School-based services are a goal if the student and/or her parents have failed to become involved in them previously.

Contracting

❏ The intervention goal can also be formalized through a behavioral contract. In utilizing this type of goal, the intervention team describes its minimal expectations of the student and asks for parental support and monitoring. Such contracts include expectations that the student will abstain from all use of alcohol or other drugs, will attend school, will attend all classes, will refrain from violence or other illegal behavior, and will attend a support group in the school. Contracts are effective only to the extent that parents agree to become involved in monitoring the student's compliance and to inform the school of any out-of-school contract violations. An important component of the contract is the student's agreement to seek an assessment and/or treatment if she is unable to abide by the contract.*

❏ The intervention goals above can be combined. The intervention team can decide, for example, that it wants the student to attend an in-school support group, abide by a behavioral contract, and participate in a community-based prevention/intervention program.

Parent-to-student intervention

There is one additional intervention goal which the team can consider. In many cases the parents will support any of the previous goals. It is the student who is resistant. Where parents have been powerless to affect their child's behavior there is something illegitimate about using the emotional power of this process to ask them to take a step that their child will refuse to comply with. In these cases, the intervention meeting with parents can be used to obtain their involvement in an intervention process with their student (see Appendix B).

CRITERIA FOR AN EFFECTIVE GOAL

Criteria for selecting the goal

Regardless of which goal the intervention team decides to present to parents, an effective goal will meet a number of criteria.

☛ *The goal of the intervention meeting is decided in advance.* The intervention meeting loses its emotional momentum if we use it for making a decision.

☛ *The goal must be justified by the data.* Parents must see a clear and definite connection between the nature of their child's problem and its implications for help.

☛ *The goal must be appropriate.* If drug abuse is a concern to any degree, the goal must involve a course of action designed to bring about abstinence.

---

* For a superb account of the types of behavioral contracts and their use with student and parents, see Schaefer (1987) *Choices and Consequences*, pp. 92-114.

☞ *The goal must be realistic.* A critical rule of confrontation is that it asks people to change only those behaviors which they realistically can. The goal of the intervention is not for parents to admit that there is a problem, or that the problem is drug abuse, or that their child needs help, etc. The goal of the intervention is to have parents agree to take a concrete step.

☞ *The goal must be specific.* The intervention process can break down if parents are merely asked to take vague steps (e.g., "Seek professional help"). If the goal involves community-based resources, the specific names of agencies or contact people should be presented. If it involves school-based services or contracts, these should be spelled out in brief detail.

☞ *The goal must be unanimous.* Every member of the intervention team must agree to support the same goal. The intervention meeting with parents is not the time to discuss different recommendations or differences of opinion. The purpose of meeting in advance is to resolve these differences and to arrive at a consensus. A condition of participating in the final intervention meeting is that the individual team member agrees to support only the group's goal at that time.

☞ *The goal must be student-based and data-based.* It is tempting for intervention teams at this point to select a goal which will provoke the least resistance or which parents will most easily accept. The intervention goal must be based solely upon what the student *needs.* Ensuring parents' agreement or compliance with the goal is often the role of consequences (see Chapter 10).

WORKSHEET 8.1

Worksheet 8.1, "Adolescent Assessment Service Checklist," suggests some basic criteria to look for in evaluating appropriate assessment agencies for adolescents and their parents. Referral to an agency or assessment program that satisfies most of these criteria can be an effective goal when intervening with parents.

WORKSHEET 8.2

Worksheet 8.2, the "Authorization for the Release of Information," conforms to federal confidentiality requirements. This form can be completed and signed by the student and/or her parents at the time they agree to seek help. School staff should verify age of consent regulations in their respective states. School staff may also wish to consult with local treatment and assessment programs and to utilize general consent forms which they prefer.

Worksheet 8.1
Adolescent Assessment Services Checklist

❏ **1. What is the assessment program's philosophy regarding drug use, drug abuse, and chemical dependency?** Since one of the primary purposes of assessment is to direct adolescents and their families to appropriate care, much depends on the agency's philosophical orientation. Whether or not it utilizes such language as "disease concept," an assessment agency should recognize the unique needs presented by chemical dependency and the fact that it is a primary, progressive, chronic condition. Even those services which regard drug use as a "symptom" should be sophisticated enough to determine when such a "symptom" has been elevated to the status of an autonomous pathology which will aggravate or complicate existing problems or prevent their resolution. The program should also be able to distinguish between those young people who will be able to change their behavior in response to education, improved parenting, or firmer expectations for more responsible conduct, and those who will require primary treatment for chemical dependency.

❏ **2. What is the program's philosophy regarding adolescent alcohol and other drug abuse?** Assessment programs which espouse a "responsible drinking" philosophy for underage youth, or which hold that some degree of experimentation or use of "recreational drugs" is acceptable should be avoided at all costs. There is less confusion for student, family, and school where agencies support abstinence as a norm for adolescents. There is a difference between expecting a certain degree of adolescent experimentation and actively condoning illegal, irresponsible, and often dangerous behavior. These permissive attitudes toward drug use should often prompt curiosity as to the degree of training the staff has had in AODA concepts as well as curiosity about the drug-using habits of the program's staff itself. It is a good idea to inquire about the agency's policy regarding staff alcohol/drug use.

❏ **3. What are the major components of the program's assessment process?** An appropriate assessment or drug evaluation program will involve more than a single interview with the adolescent and/or her family. It will tacitly recognize assessment as a process in which a great deal of data must be collected from a variety of sources. A good assessment program will also include an alcohol/drug education component for the adolescent as well as for family members.

❏ **4. Does the program require parent/family involvement?** The diagnostic or evaluation judgements of a program are only as sound as the collected data upon which they are based. Therefore, if either the family or the school system is ignored, two of the most important sources of information will be lost. The assessment process will either be prolonged, or the staff are likely to return evaluations of "no chemical dependency" based on inadequate data.

❏ **5. What is the length of the assessment process?** A formal assessment program, as opposed to an agency that advertises an "assessment service," will be structured over a period of time. Many programs are organized into "phases" which involve an intake procedure, an education component, individual counseling, conjoint student/family sessions, group counseling, etc.

❏ **6. What range of assessment/diagnostic judgements does the program and/or its staff recognize (e.g., "abuse," "dependency," "high risk without abstinence," etc.)?** To be valuable to the student, the family, and the school as assessment program will offer a broad range of evaluative judgements between the two extremes of "no drug problem" and "is chemically dependent and needs inpatient treatment." It should be capable of assessing the adolescent's strengths and weaknesses and those of his environment in order to ascertain how supportive of change that environment will be. The program should also be able to recommend a wide range of courses of action appropriate to a range of diagnostic judgements supported by the data it collects.

❏ **7. What is the staffing pattern?** Does the adolescent and/or the family interact with more than one person? In general, the more individuals who have an opportunity to see and work with an adolescent and his family, the greater will be the depth of the assessment.

❏ **8. What is the process for admission to the program?** A good rule of thumb is to refer to a person, not to a program or an agency. It is advisable to identify those who see the student and/or family members first, and those counselors or therapists who seem most accepted by and successful with adolescents. There is nothing wrong with telling students and families to "insist on seeing Ms. Jones" if she does the most trustworthy work.

❏ **9. What is the nature of the working relationship between the assessment agency or service and the school system?** The agency should be eager to establish not only referral relationships but day-to-day working relationships as well. An effective assessment program or service will appreciate the amount of information the school can contribute to the assessment process and the degree of support the latter can provide for the student engaged in making healthy changes in his behavior. It will not irrationally assert "confidentiality" when approached by the school, but will routinely seek releases of information in order to enable staff to communicate with the school system. It will also assist the school in seeking such releases of information from families when the school refers them to the agency.

❏ **10. Will the agency provide the school with technical assistance?** Many assessment agencies will provide staff or services to the school, ranging from inservices and training programs to school-based assessment services and support group leadership. The school should inquire about the agency's ability to assist it in the process of preparing for and conducting interventions with students and/or parents.

❏ **11. Is the agency specifically approved, licensed, and/or certified by the state to provide alcohol/drug services?** While many agencies in a given community may present themselves as assessment resources, not all will have the expertise or experience in dealing appropriately and competently with alcohol and other drug-related problems. Not all alcohol/drug -specific agencies are adept at working with adolescents. All things considered, however, those agencies which are subject to regular survey by the state for compliance with state mandates for alcohol/drug services should be preferred over general counseling centers, mental health centers, or private practitioners in alcohol/drug abuse matters.

❏ **12. What are the qualifications of the staff? Are they certified alcohol/drug counselors?** What is the experience of the staff in working specifically with adolescent alcohol/drug problems? Alcohol and/or drug certification and experience in working with drug-involved youth should be the two minimum qualifications of the staff in any program or agency offering adolescent AODA assessment services to the school. The formal certification process at least assures that the counselor or therapist has satisfied the minimum educational, skill, and practicum requirements of the state certification body. Experience in working with adolescent as opposed to adult drug abusers enhances the counselor's appreciation of the unique problems presented by the interaction between drug abuse and adolescent development.

❏ **13. Does the assessment agency also operate a residential or outpatient program for the primary treatment of chemical dependency?** Does the agency refer clients to other treatment programs? How many such referrals have taken place in the past year? If the assessment program also provides primary treatment for chemical dependency it is wise to inquire about its diagnostic and referral statistics. Diagnosing a high percentage of incoming clients as chemically dependent can be a reflection of a bias. (It can just as easily indicate that the agency receives a disproportionately high number of referrals of young people who are likely to be heavily involved with alcohol or other drugs). Similarly, referring to one's own treatment program when others are accessible or comparable in cost may also reflect a conflict of interest. The fact is, no ten adolescents will benefit equally from the same program. The treatment field has evolved sufficiently to provide a wide range of programs suited to individual differences in adolescent patients.

❏ **14. To what other agencies or services does the assessment program refer?** For example, how many adolescents were referred to Alcoholics Anonymous, Narcotics Anonymous, Cocaine Anonymous, to other therapists in the community, to the school's services, etc.? A good assessment program will recognize that adolescents and families will frequently have many more problems than those presented by alcohol or drug abuse alone. It will also appreciate the value of self-help groups in the community for both the adolescent and his family.

❏ **15. What is the cost of the assessment program?** Is the program eligible to receive third-party insurance payments? Are fees based upon ability to pay? Assessment programs will vary in their services, their funding sources, and in their fee systems. Publicly funded programs are often free, at least in part, or have a nominal fee for services beyond a set number of sessions. Even private agencies seek third-party payments and arrange for public assistance for families in financial need. It is necessary for the school to have such information at hand when referring families to assessment services.*

---

*Adapted from Anderson (1988), *When Chemicals Come to School*, pp. 159-161. Used by permission.

Worksheet 8.2
Authorization For Release of Information

General Consent Form

I, _____ ,

(student name)

authorize _____

(name of person/school /agency disclosing information)

to disclose to _____

(name or title of person/organization to whom information is to be disclosed)

the following identifying information from my records: *(specify the extent or nature of information to be disclosed)*

_____
_____
_____
_____
_____

The purpose or need for such disclosure is: _____
_____
_____

I understand that my records are protected under the federal regulations governing Confidentiality of Alcohol and Drug Abuse Patient Records, 42 CFR Part 2, and cannot be disclosed without my written consent unless otherwise provided for in the regulations. I also understand that I may revoke this consent at any time except to the extent that action has been taken in reliance on it, and that in any event this consent expires automatically as follows: _____
_____

(specify date or condition upon which this consent expires)

SIGNATURE OF STUDENT: _____ DATE: _____

SIGNATURE OF WITNESS: _____ DATE: _____

SIGNATURE OF PARENT/
GUARDIAN, LEGAL REP: _____ DATE: _____

CHAPTER NINE

UNHOOKING

Denial is a statement about an individual;
resistance is a statement about a relationship.
Resistance takes two.

Each intervention team member will, during the intervention meeting with parents, share with them selected items of data. When everyone has shared their behaviors of concern, the facilitator will state the goal that the group has decided upon. He will ask if parents will comply with it ("Will you...?"), and await their response. A parent will often react to individual team members' data with minimizing, rationalizing, explaining, justifying, or any of the other forms which denial may take. Faced at the end of the intervention meeting with a difficult decision to make, parents often react with even stronger resistance.

One of the key preparation steps is "unhooking," or anticipating the forms which parent denial may take, and preparing responses which avoid participating in their denial during the intervention meeting. The emotional and cognitive power which the team has been able to utilize can dissipate as it or its members begin reacting to each statement parents make as they resist getting help. The more the group allows the focus to be deflected away from the "Will you...?" decision, the less likely the intervention is to be successful. The process of unhooking involves understanding the difference between parents' *objections*, parents' *resistance*, and parents' *refusal* to get help. It also involves preparing individual and group responses to each of these in advance of the intervention meeting.

ANTICIPATING PARENT OBJECTIONS

Emotional surrender

Objections represent real, tangible, practical, concrete, and solvable problems. The most important thing to understand about a parent's objections is that they are not refusals to get help for his student. They most often indicate an *emotional surrender*—the parent has recognized at an emotional level the appropriateness of the team's recommendation and is willing to go along with it. The objections often represent weak though important forms of denial. They often begin with "But what about..." or "We can't do that because...".

Prepare solutions

It is important for the intervention team to try to predict in advance, based on what they know about the student and his parents, what forms these objections may take and to list them on paper. The next step is to prepare solutions and to list each of them as well. These solutions are shared during the intervention meeting only when the parent raises a particular objection. The solution can be shared by the facilitator or by the team member to whom each is relevant.

Objections to Assessment or Treatment

If the goal is for participation in an assessment or treatment program, many parent objections take the form of questions about these:

- ❑ *"What will that cost? We can't afford it"*
- ❑ *"What happens to you there?"*
- ❑ *"Do we have to participate?"*
- ❑ *"How long does it last?"*

Here it is vital that the facilitator have specific information about each of the assessment or treatment programs that might be recommended. If a professional alcohol/drug abuse counselor has been included on the team they can be helpful in answering these types of questions.

Here are some sample objections involving assessment or treatment and some examples of possible solutions to them:

- ❑ *"What if they say nothing is wrong?"* ('We will be forwarding our data to the agency as well. Our data clearly shows that something is wrong. Will you...?')

- ❑ *"What if they say he is an addict?"* ('The assessment agency will recommend an appropriate treatment program. Will you...?')

- ❑ *"We've already tried that."* ('These facts show that things have gotten worse and a new assessment is justified. Will you..." or 'Many kids don't respond well the first time they are in treatment. His current pattern of drug abuse requires additional professional help to interrupt. Will you...?').

Notice that following each response the parent's attention is refocussed on the decision by "Will you...".

Other Objections

Assessment or treatment may not be the issue triggering parent objections. Almost any intervention goal will disrupt the status quo. This disruption is the source of many objection statement. Because objections are so unique to each student and his family, it is impossible to predict all of them here. The following is a list of some other areas concerning which the team can anticipate objections, along with some representative solutions:

❏ *"But he'll lose his job."* ('It is illegal for him to be fired for getting treatment. He *can* be fired for failing to show up for work, or continuing to come to work 'high.' Will you...?')

❏ *"But what will people say?"* ('This meeting is confidential. Nothing about this meeting will leave this room. Treatment and assessment programs are also bound by strict confidentiality laws. For now, you can just tell people that he is seeing a professional to sort out some problems. Will you...?')

The solutions to some parent objections will involve school policies: athletics and other extracurricular activities, credit for treatment, etc.

❏ *"But he's already missed so much school."* ('Unless things change he is likely to miss more. We want to help you stop that. The treatment program has teachers on staff, and we will help him stay current in his classes. We also give credit for things he accomplishes in treatment. So, will you...?')

❏ *"But what if he doesn't graduate."* (Similar to above)

❏ *"But we can't have this on his record."* ('Nothing about this meeting, his assessment, or treatment ever becomes a part of his educational records. Prospective employers, colleges, etc., will never know anything about this unless he tells them. So, will you...?')

❏ *"But he'll get kicked off the football team."* ('Because of his current drug abuse he is ineligible as of now. Our policy states that if he completes treatment satisfactorily and stays drug-free there is no reason why he can't have all the privileges of other students. So, will you...?)

❏ *"But he'll never agree to go."* ('We can help you organize a formal intervention which we are all willing to participate in. They are nearly always successful. So, will you...?')

Each of these objections raises a real issue which has a real, concrete solution. Objections should not be seen, therefore, as deflections which should be ignored, but as evidence of an emotional surrender. It merely remains for the intervention team member to supply a brief solution and then to refocus the parent's attention on the decision to seek help.

ANTICIPATING PARENT RESISTANCE

Resistance requires two

Like objections, resistance can indicate an emotional surrender simply because it does not consist of a clear "No!" Resistance, however, is an entirely different phenomenon which requires an entirely different response from intervention team members. Resistance describes an interrelationship: it requires two people. Resistance, for example, requires that one person blames and that another reacts by blaming back or defending himself in some other way. Anger and blame can also trigger emotional or physical withdrawal. They can also trigger "placating:" a response by someone else which is designed to keep the level of conflict low (e.g., "There's no need to raise our voices," etc.).

These behaviors are the ego defenses described in Chapter 2 and listed in Figure 2.1 on pages 10-11. An ego defense becomes a form of resistance when it begins to manipulate another's behavior by triggering an ego defense in them. We begin to resist the resistance. A parent's resistance is strengthened when the intervenor adds his defenses to it by *reacting* rather than *responding*. The intervention can degenerate into an argument, or the team may feel so threatened or frustrated that it will back away from its facts, its goal, or its consequences.

The task of the intervention team members, then, is *to anticipate* those forms which a parent's resistance may take, *to identify* how they usually react when confronted by these behaviors, and *to prepare* a different and more effective response.

Anticipating Resistance and Team Reactions

Unless a team member knows the parents well or has had previous experiences with them it will be difficult for him to predict with any certainty how they will react to the confrontation. In general, parents will react in four different ways, similar to those listed in Figure 2.1.

Being Super-rational

Some parents will react to the emotional power of the facts, the school's recommendation, or the intervention itself by being "super-rational." They will greet the intervenor's data with questions, intellectualizations and justifications, or with minimizing and excusing, or with explanations. Each of these are marked by their focus on rationality. If the level of interaction can be lifted away from the painful to the emotionless and abstract, the parent can avoid the emotional power of the intervention. If team members join him on this super-rational plain by debating or attempting to discount the parent's abstractions, they will be strengthening his resistance and losing their emotional power.

Withdrawing

Other parents may react to the intervention by appearing to withdraw. They sit in silence, they don't make eye-contact, or they look at the floor. They may appear sad and depressed. Or, they may make deflecting and distracting comments which have nothing to do with what is going on (e.g., "It was hard to get here on time with all the traffic"). One common reaction to withdrawing behaviors is to redouble efforts: team members start asking loaded questions to engage the parent's attention (e.g., "Is any of this getting through? Am I making any sense?"). Team members often become frustrated and then angry in response to a parent's apparent disinterest. Parents' silence can also imply fragility. Team members can participate in this resistance by withholding painful incidents as they share their data or by backing away from their goal ("Maybe treatment isn't necessary") or by reducing their consequences. In any event, "getting hooked" by this form of resistance can severely reduce the impact of the confrontation.

"Placating," or being compliant

Some parents may react to the intervention with a studied pleasantness. They may joke, flatter various team members, or interrupt with long monologues. Rather than denying the team member's facts they may constantly nod in agreement with all of them. They will sometimes react with apparent compliance: e.g., "We'll make sure he gets here on time from now on," "You're right. We'll forbid him to use the car the next time he gets drunk." Compliance is meant to minimize conflict by giving lip service to the facts. It signals parents' unwillingness to face the emotional pain of what is happening to their child. Team members might react to compliance with frustration and anger, as they would to withdrawal. They feel like they are not being heard. Another reaction matches compliance with compliance. When sharing data, team members can interpret a parents' agreeableness as evidence that he is at last willing to take some action. They can consequently omit important data. Faced with this apparent compliance, the facilitator might be tempted to cut the intervention short, announcing the goal without letting everyone on the team speak and preventing the steady accumulation of data from doing its emotional work.

Anger, blame, and hostility

Perhaps the most common reaction of parents—and the one about which team members are the most phobic—is hostility. As team members share their data they can be met with anger, blame, threats, sarcasm, verbal abuse, or physical acting-out (e.g., banging fists on the table). Parent anger is most often countered either with a team member's own anger, blame, and self-defense, or with withdrawal and "backing down." Threats of legal action are both common and commonly effective at deflecting the team from its data, its goal, and its consequences.

Identifying Team Members' Reactions

Facilitator's role

Team members should be prepared to expect anything from parents in reaction to the intervention. Helping intervention team members to discover how they might "get hooked," or react to parents' defenses is another key task of the intervention facilitator. During this phase of preparation the facilitator can help identify these reactions through questions (see Worksheet 9.1):

❑ How have the parents reacted in other similar contexts (if the team member has had previous experience)?

❑ How did the team member react at the time? What happened?

❏ What can parents say or do that will be the most uncomfortable to witness?

❏ How can parents "get to you?"

❏ What is the worst you fear will happen during the intervention?

Potential parent resistance can also be anticipated as the team rehearses for the intervention meeting through roleplaying (see Chapter 11).

Preparing Effective Responses

It is important that team members see parent reactions as self-protective and that they accept and respect these behaviors as such. Alanon has used the term "detachment" for what we have called "unhooking:" separating from the behavior, not the person. One way of seeing parent resistance differently involves taking an emotional step back from it, as if it were a picture, and learning to admire it. We ask ourselves questions like "What is going on here?" and "What is this doing for the person?" and "What is really going on inside?"

One of the pitfalls in intervening is assuming that parent reactions to what we are saying and doing are accurate. It often helps to visualize the interaction as in Figure 9.1. The parent can be seen as having a considerable amount of emotional pain (about what has been happening to him and his child, as well as about the intervention meeting) covered up by well-practiced denial behaviors and ego defenses. What we are saying *is heard* by

Figure 9.1

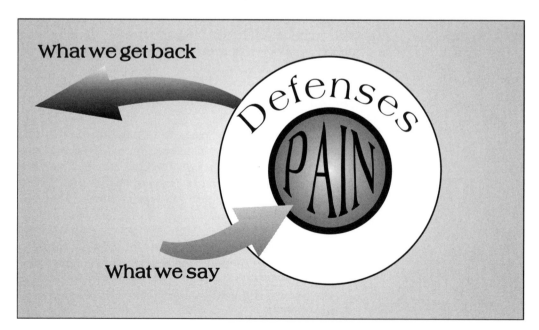

this painful part, but the feedback we get is from the denial system. Hence, a parent's reaction is not accurate feedback for the intervenor. For him to take it literally is to allow the denial system to guide the intervention. If team members can learn how not to take parents' comments personally or literally they can avoid getting hooked by them and losing the emotional momentum of the intervention meeting.

Responses to parent resistance

If team members are not to react to parents' reactions, how should they respond? Just as it is not possible here to list all of the possible forms that parent resistance might take, it is not possible to provide a detailed list of recommended responses to it. There are, however, two general classes of appropriate responses to parent resistance. The first is *silence.* Silence acknowledges the parent's resistance by not trying to interrupt it, deflect it, react to it, counteract it, etc. Silence allows the parent to expend the physical energy that is supporting the resistant behavior. As the parent rages, for example, the team member sits quietly until the parent is finished. After prolonging the silence a bit he continues where he left off if the parent interrupted him. Silence protects parents and team members alike from escalating debates, shouting matches, and arguments. The team's silence carries a message. It says "This is serious," "We will not deny your denial," and it says "I am not going to be deflected from my goal."

Silence

Joining

Another category of responses consists of "joining" parents, or acknowledging and accepting whatever validity attaches to their feelings or statements without being deflected by them.

> ☞ "I know it is difficult to hear some of this. But, you need to know that (data)..."

> ☞ "You have every right to be angry about what has been happening."

> ☞ "I know you want what is best for your child. That is why we are recommending...(goal)"

In any event, the individual team member can ask himself the following questions as he identifies specific alternative responses to parents:

> ❑ How am I *automatically* inclined to *react* when a parent does/says X?

> ❑ How will I *respond* instead during the intervention meeting?

ANTICIPATING PARENT REFUSAL

Parent objections or resistance usually indicate some degree of emotional surrender to the intervention process, especially if they occur after parents have been presented with the goal and asked to comply with it. It is thus important for the team to have prepared in advance answers to questions and responses to deflections so that parents' attention can be kept focussed on the decision to get appropriate help. The team must also be prepared, however, for parents' *refusal* to support the intervention goal, whether it is assessment, treatment, or some other option. Refusal differs from objections or resistance in two key ways. First, where objections and resistance can appear to be refusals but have a "yes" buried within them, the refusal to acquiesce in the team's intervention goal is typically a clear and unmistakable "No!" A parent might react, for example, with:

> *"This is the last straw! We are tired of having the school gang up on our child. If you guys were doing your job none of this would have happened. There is no way we are going to any drug agency. You can expect to hear from our attorney!"*

Secondly, the appropriate response to a firm refusal is not to argue or to summon additional facts or reasons. The appropriate response by the team to a parent's refusal is to begin listing the consequences of their child's failure to change or their refusal to seek help for him. Thus, the next preparation task is to determine these consequences in advance.

WORKSHEET 9.1

The facilitator can utilize Worksheet 9.1, "Anticipating Denial," to help team members identify and prepare responses to objections and resistance. Before completing the worksheet, team members will need some background information on the difference between objections and resistance and some examples of each.

Team members can be given the worksheet as "homework" during the preparation process (see Appendix C). Upon reconvening, the facilitator can assist team members in identifying appropriate responses to resistance, and the group can make whatever arrangements are necessary to enact the solutions to parent objections.

Worksheet 9.1
Anticipating Denial

Intervention Goal(s):

Objections. Objections are usually tangible, solvable problems or obstacles which parents see as standing in the way of agreeing with the intervention goal. It is important to anticipate and prepare solutions to as many of these as possible. *On the left, list as many ways as you can in which parents might object to following through with the goal, above. On the right, list as many realistic solutions to each objection as you can.*

OBJECTION	SOLUTION

MORE ||||➡

RESISTANCE. Resistance can be thought of as a defensive behavior which is designed to provoke a defensive reaction in others, diverting them from their purpose. Unlike objections or obstacles, resistance does not present problems to be solved but behaviors to which a *response*—rather than a *reaction*—is required. Intervenors need to anticipate what forms parent resistance is likely to take and to develop non-reactive responses to them. Your answers to the following questions can help you identify some forms which parent resistance might take.

RESISTANCE:	APPROPRIATE RESPONSE(S) *(To be completed with the help of the intervention facilitator and the intervention team)*
1. My greatest fear about what might happen during the intervention meeting is:	
2. A parent can almost always "get to" me by (saying/doing):	
3. I will want to get up and leave during the intervention if:	
4. When I introduce myself, parents are likely to react with:	
5. The data I will share that is most likely to provoke parents is:	
6. I will know the intervention is going to fail if:	
7. I will not want to continue sharing my data if parents:	
8. Others?	

CHAPTER TEN

DECIDING ON CONSEQUENCES

The intervention team should be prepared for the possibility that parents will refuse to seek appropriate help for their child or to acquiesce in the school's goal. It is important to be emotionally prepared for this eventuality: all of the preparation that has gone into the intervention might seem to be for nothing. It can be argued, however, that interventions always succeed to some degree if they are well-prepared. At the very least, the parents as well as the intervention team members have much more information than they did before and have a clearer idea of what must change. An intervention will always have some impact on the denial system of everyone involved. Moreover, the intervention that appears to fail may lay the ground work for the success of the next one.

If parents should fail to agree with the team's goal the team members need to have considered the consequences of this failure. Team members need to develop in advance a set of consequences: what will happen if the student' behavior fails to change or worsens and what will happen if parents fail to seek appropriate help. While the intervention goal is the result of a group consensus, the consequences should be individual and written out. In this phase of preparation the team considers what are appropriate consequences.

Consequences are a necessary component of the intervention because they address the issue of enabling, the essence of which is the absence of consequences for the student's behavior. Those surrounding the student have often done things or failed to do things which have prevented her from experiencing the consequences of her behavior. Parents also may have been enabled by being protected from the consequences of their child's behavior or their own. The message of the intervention meeting is that this will now change.

INAPPROPRIATE CONSEQUENCES

In preparing consequences, the facilitator essentially asks the intervention team *"What will you do if the parents refuse to support getting help? What will you no longer do?"* As team members begin brainstorming lists of consequences the facilitator should help evaluate them for appropriateness. Not all consequences are appropriate or effective. Appropriate consequences must **not** be:

❏ *Empty threats:* things people have threatened to do in past but did not do, or did not followed through with for long;

❏ *Punishments:* punishments are designed to inflict pain or harm and can be unrelated to the behavior. The statement of punitive goals only increases parent denial rather than reducing it;

❏ *Bargains or sacrifices:* bargaining says 'If you do this, I'll do that.' It makes the individual's behavior contingent on a parent's behavior. Bargains almost always lessen consequences. What appears on the surface to be good motivation (*"If you agree to get your student treatment I'll forget the expulsion"*) is in fact very enabling. Sacrifices involve giving something up in return for an agreement to get help. Sacrifices by definition require the team member to suffer a consequence, not the student or parent (*"I'll spend extra time with them after school;" "I'll let her continue to play on the volley-ball team, despite the school's policy"*). These are consequences characteristic of codependency.

❏ *Enabling:* statements of consequences need to be evaluated to see if any aspect of them contributes to the enabling around the student or her parents;

❏ *Collective:* appropriate consequences are based on the individual experience which each team member has with the student or her parents. When expressed individually such consequences are infinitely more impactful than a list of consequences endorsed by the group. "I" statements are more effective than "we" statements.

> **Good consequences are NOT:**
>
> ☛ **Empty threats**
> ☛ **Punishments**
> ☛ **Bargains**
> ☛ **Sacrifices**
> ☛ **Enabling**
> ☛ **Collective**

APPROPRIATE CONSEQUENCES

Natural and logical

Appropriate consequences are, in general, *natural* and/or *logical* A consequence is natural if it inevitably grows out of the behavior by itself. A hangover, for example, is a natural consequence of overuse of alcohol or other drugs. Many of a student's problems may stem naturally from her alcohol/drug abuse. Logical consequences, as the term implies, follow logically from behavior but usually require some kind of intervention by others. Missing school, for example, could result in an arrest for truancy; failing to keep up with household chores or to abide by rules at home could result in a loss of privileges; drug abuse at work could result in job action. In any case, if a consequence is natural and logical it is connected directly to behavior in a way that a punishment is not. Appropriate consequences help students and parents to make decisions better. The absence of consequences deprives either of information they need if they are to decide to act differently in the future.

Effective Consequences ARE:

☑ **Natural and/or logical**
☑ **Things people are committed to doing**
☑ **Things people are able to do**
☑ **Assertions of team members' rights to be happy, healthy, and safe**
☑ **Non-enabling**
☑ **Individualized**

In addition to being natural, logical, and avoiding the pitfalls above, an effective consequence for intervention should meet several criteria. An effective consequence:

❑ Represents something the team member is *willing to do.* Only those consequences should be expressed which the team member is committed to following through with. In identifying consequences, team members need to anticipate the logical outcomes of taking a course of action. A principal, for example, should not assert expulsion as a consequence for a student unless she has anticipated and committed herself to following-through with the various legal and policy steps required.

❑ Represents something the team member is *able to do.* An individual may not be able—legally, physically, emotionally, etc.—to carry out steps they are otherwise willing to do. The school may be willing to expel a student but may not have the legal or policy basis for doing so. A peer may be willing to terminate her friendship with the student but may not be emotionally capable of telling her so. The language used to express consequences must take the "willing and able" criteria into account. Strictly speaking, a principal may not be able to expel but may be able to recommend expulsion to the school board.

❏ Represents an a*ssertion of someone's rights to be healthy, happy, and safe.* Effective consequences are designed to have an impact on student and parent behavior, but they are also evidence of "unhooking." Team members essentially assert that it has become unpleasant, unhealthy or unsafe for them to be around the student's behavior as it is. The classroom teacher, for example, has a right to a climate that fosters learning in her classroom. The student's behavior constitutes a threat to that climate for the teacher and other students—unless the student changes or agrees to get help, she will no longer be in that class.

❏ *Is non-enabling:* it says that the student and/or parent will not be protected from the natural and logical consequences of her behavior.

❏ *Is individualized.* Consequences expressed as "we" statements can contribute to parents' feeling of being 'ganged up on.' Individual consequences minimize these feelings. Hearing many different consequences expressed from team members representing many areas of their child's life helps parents to see the magnitude of the problems that *will result* if the student does not get help or if they refuse to support it.

TYPES OF CONSEQUENCES

Effective consequences must be developed in two areas: (1) consequences for the student's failure to change her behavior, and (2) consequences for the parents' unwillingness to support the intervention team's goal.

Student-based consequences

Student-based consequences should be related to the data which team members have collected. The last column of Worksheet 7.3, for example, asks team members to identify what they did of an enabling nature in response to a student's behavior. The range of consequences will be related to the diversity and range of the members of the intervention team. Ideally, consequences could be developed in each of the areas discussed in Chapter 5 (pp. 34-36). A good way of discovering appropriate consequences, then, is to ask "What will I do differently next time?" Many of these consequences are, then, *predictive:* they spell out what *will* happen if the behavior continues.

Predictive consequences

Motivational consequences

Behavior which has resulted in illegal activity or the violation of key school policies can invoke a *motivational* consequence. In this situation the parent is told the earned consequence of the student's current or past behavior. For example, the violation of the policies against in-school drug abuse has *earned* the student a recommendation for expulsion. Or, drug-dealing has *earned* the student a one-year prison sentence. A motivational consequence can reduce the earned consequence in recognition of future responsible behavior. Thus, a principal could say that she will hold in abeyance a recommendation for expulsion if the student gets an assessment for drug abuse and complies with the assessor's recommendations. Similarly, a juvenile justice worker could state that she will recommend to the judge a reduced sentence if the student completes treatment and stays drug-free for one year. (Motivational consequences sound suspiciously like bargains. While a bargain *withholds* a consequence, a motivational consequence *imposes* it but rewards the student and/or her parents for complying successfully with the intervention goal.)

Appropriate parent-based consequences are more difficult to develop. Sometimes the natural, logical consequences of a child's failure to change will impact upon parents. Many communities, for example, are more vigorously enforcing truancy ordinances. An unending course of truancy arrests will compel parents to attend a continual series of court appearances. In other communities parents are being held legally and financially liable for the conduct of their minor child. The "able" criterion above states that only those consequences should be expressed which members of the team can legally carry out. To avoid being punitive, parent-based consequences must reflect a team member's legitimate sphere of influence regarding parents.

Child abuse

Finally, consider the case where the school has reasonable evidence of a student's chemical dependency. This evidence can be the result of the data collected by school staff (see Chapter 7). Or, a student may have already been assessed or diagnosed as chemically dependent by a community agency, but the student and/or parents have refused to comply with a request for treatment. Under these circumstances a serious case could be made for child abuse or neglect in many states. If a parent has refused to agree with the team's goal of assessment or treatment, consider the impact of the principal who states:

> *"I'm very sorry to hear that. However, we have evidence that your child is chemically dependent. Chemical dependency is an illness which is ultimately fatal without appropriate treatment. Under state statute, your failure to seek the appropriate help constitutes an extreme form of child abuse and neglect. Therefore, if I do not hear within 48 hours that you have admitted your child to a treatment program, I am required by law to file a report for child abuse."*

Role of the facilitator

The role of the facilitator at this stage is to educate team members concerning the nature of conequences, to assist them in identifying consequences, to evaluate them for appropriateness, and to insure that everyone on the team is aware of everyone else's consequences.

WORKSHEET 10.1

The facilitator can utilize Worksheet 10.1 to summarize the consequences of the team for herself. This can be a useful reminder if, during the intervention meeting, someone forgets or misstates their consequences. If the intervention ends in a parent refusal, a copy can also be given to parents.

Worksheet 10.1
Consequences Summary Sheet

Team Member	Relationship to Student	Consequence(s) For Student	Consequence(s) For Parent(s)

CHAPTER ELEVEN

PLANNING THE AGENDA

All of the preparation that has occurred thus far can be eroded if equal attention is not given to the structure of the intervention meeting itself. A host of specific, strategic questions arise as the team begins to anticipate the intervention session: Will we all participate? Who will chair the meeting? How do we say the things we have prepared? What if we get interrupted? When will we hold the meeting? How will we get parents to come? It is important that the meeting *have* a structure and that all team members understand it in advance. Consequently, to prepare for the final meeting with parents the team must accomplish the following tasks:

❑   Select the final intervention team
❑   Select a person to moderate the intervention meeting
❑   Determine the order of speaking
❑   Review the agenda and rehearse the meeting
❑   Plan how to convene parents

SELECTING THE FINAL TEAM

Time constraints

Time is one of the constraints on the intervention team. Most effective intervention meetings need not last longer than one hour. Therefore, not all of the data that has been collected can be shared. Another constraint is voluntarism. It is crucial that participation on the intervention team be

Voluntary participation

completely voluntary. This is especially important with regard to the student's peers, siblings or other family members. It is not necessary for everyone who has been a part of the preliminary team to take part in the intervention session. Some individuals drop out as the preparation process unfolds. Others may be willing to help in the preparation but may not be willing to take part in the confrontation meeting.

Criteria for selecting the team

While there are no definite rules, six to eight participants is perhaps optimal. More than eight participants would lengthen the meeting significantly. Fewer than six participants may not have sufficient data to be impactful. In identifying the final intervention team, care should be taken to select individuals:

➤ *Who have the most impactful data* to share concerning the student's behavior. The team will have collected far more data than is possible to relate. Care must be taken both to select only two or three of the most meaningful incidents and to identify those individuals whose data is likely to be the most convincing to parents.

➤ *Who have effective consequences.* While everyone who has first-hand information will be able to generate a consequence, some consequences will be more impactful than others.

➤ *Who are clearly committed to supporting the same goal.* The last thing we want to happen during the intervention meeting is for team members to begin second-guessing each other or debating among themselves concerning alternative recommendation for help.

➤ *Who have the most significant relationship to the student and/or parents.* There may be several individuals for whom parents have more respect, whose opinions they trust, or who have had a good relationship with their student in some way in the past.

➤ *Who are least likely to "get hooked."* It is possible that someone on the preliminary team may have excellent data but may also have been seriously harmed by the student's conduct and who may be unable remain sufficiently detached emotionally during the intervention. He might decide to restrict his participation in some way, or not to participate at all.

The facilitator can make his recommendations, based on these criteria, and solicit suggestions as to the final makeup of the intervention team.

SELECTING A "MODERATOR"

Someone will have to chair the intervention session with parents. Since an intervention meeting is not a therapy session, the leader need not be a therapist or counselor. Nor is the moderator necessarily the same person who has been facilitating the preparation process. The choice of the moderator is not based on his credentials, but on a number of practical considerations.

➤ *The moderator's role is voluntary.* As the person chairing the meeting, he may be the focus of much of parents' initial resistance. The person selected to chair the meeting should be willing to place himself in this unpopular position and should be able to deal with it effectively.

➤ *The moderator should not be provocative.* An effective moderator is someone who may have had a good relationship with parents in the past, or someone who they trust and respect, or someone who is emotionally neutral with respect to them and the situation.

➤ *The moderator can be an authority figure.* A principal, juvenile justice official, or someone else in a position of authority respecting the student can be a good choice (subject to the previous condition).

➤ *The moderator can be someone who parents trust or respect.* If a teacher, counselor, coach, or clergyman has had a positive relationship with the student or the family in the past, or has the respect of parents or the student, he can function effectively in the moderator's role.

➤ *The moderator can be an alcohol/drug professional from the community.* An alcohol/drug counselor or other therapist can be an effective moderator. He has the advantage of being emotionally neutral if he has no previous experience with the student or family. Alcohol/drug professionals can answer many parent questions and concerns accurately and are likely to be experienced in the intervention process.

The moderator's role   The moderator's role during the intervention meeting consists of several basic tasks: (1) to greet the parents when they enter the meeting; (2) to introduce intervention team members; (3) to state the purpose of the meeting; (4) to secure a commitment to abide by the meeting's ground rules, and (5) to keep the meeting focussed (see Chapter 12).

DECIDING ON AN ORDER

One way in which parents can deflect team members or the intervention meeting as a whole is to interrupt, ask questions, or turn their attention away from one speaker and attempt to engage someone else. The person who can decide who will speak next will have all of the power in the intervention meeting. Parents—or more accurately, the denial system—will have this power unless the intervention team reserves it to itself. The team can retain this power by deciding in advance on an explicit "1,2,3..." order to speak in and by agreeing to stick to that order no matter what. If interrupted they will pause and continue after a silence. If asked a question, they will not respond if it is not their turn ("unhooking," Chapter 9).

An effective order is determined by the nature of team members' relationship to the student and/or parents and by their data. In general, the least provocative person(s) speak first as the team tries to build trust and rapport. The most provocative person goes in the middle after some trust has been established. The person with the most emotionally impactful data, or who has the most intimate relationship with parents speaks near the end. Information concerning drug abuse is very last, when parent denial is weakened and they are most receptive to difficult information.

REVIEWING AND REHEARSING THE AGENDA

The facilitator should also review the agenda with the team and practice it at least once before the intervention session with parents. The following brief review of the agenda is described in more detail in Chapter 12:

The agenda

1. The moderator will greet parents when they arrive and will introduce members of the intervention team. He will state the purpose of the meeting and secure the group's commitment to the major ground rule (see p. 88).

2. Each member of the team will, in turn, share two or three of his most significant facts regarding the student's behaviors of concern. He may ask parents if they have noticed anything of concern to them as well. Facts concerning the student's alcohol or other drug abuse will be shared last.

3. The moderator (or another designated person) will state the group's goal and ask if parents are willing to support it. Parents' objections or questions will be responded to and followed immediately with "Will you...".

4. If parents clearly refuse, the group will go around a second time, in order, sharing their consequences.

5. If parents still refuse, the moderator will summarize consequences and adjourn the meeting. If parents accept the referral advice, they will meet with one or more people after the meeting to make arrangements.

6. As soon after the meeting as possible the team will meet to "debrief:" processing feelings, agreeing on consequences, clarifying the follow-up process, etc.

Rehearsal

The intervention team should rehearse the agenda at least once. It is advisable to ask someone to play the role of the parent(s) during the rehearsal. If the "stand-ins" know the parents or have had previous experience with them they will be able to portray more accurately the kind of reactions the team can expect. They should enact various types of objections, resistance, and refusal. This allows the team members to identify "hooks" they might not have anticipated, to practice responses to objections and resistance, and to practice presenting consequences. The rehearsal provides team members with confidence and practice. It also brings to the foreground anything that might go wrong that has not been anticipated. It provides team members with what is probably their last chance to ask questions about the process or to make changes in their data, the order, consequences, etc.

CONVENING THE PARENTS

If at all possible it is important for both custodial parents to attend the intervention session. If only one parent participates in the intervention, and then takes the information home, he is faced with counteracting the other parent's denial alone. His agreement with the goal is very likely to be undermined by the other parent, by the student, or both.

Where to meet

Scheduling the intervention session entails making decisions about where and when to meet and how to get parents to attend. If the school has been the major force in orchestrating the intervention, a school site will most often be the logical place to meet: a principal's office, counselor's office, conference room, board room, etc. If it is impossible to get parents to meet at the school, alternatives can be chosen: a clergyman's office, the courthouse, a social worker or therapist's office, etc. (It is rarely advisable to hold the intervention meeting in the home).

From the beginning, team members may have been doubtful about getting the parents to attend the intervention session. There are a number of strategies which have been shown to be effective.

Invitation letter

A good first strategy is to simply invite parents to the meeting with a letter, followed by a telephone call. The letter should come from someone in authority in the school, usually the principal. The letter may also originate with another official if the intervention is being held under the auspices of another institution (e.g., the juvenile justice system). The person inviting parents to the meeting should be a member of the intervention team, or at least have participated in the preliminaries. The letter essentially states that a number of people have noticed certain behaviors of concern, that the school wishes to share these with parents and to agree on a course of action. The letter states that it will be followed-up by a confirming telephone call. In that call, the sender verifies the parents' receipt of the letter and schedules the meeting. The sender should avoid getting into details of the student's case beyond what the letter might include, or the temptation to begin the intervention over the phone.

If parents refuse

Parents' adamant or repeated refusal to attend any meeting with the school is not uncommon, especially if their child has a history of chronic problems in behavior, discipline, or academic performance. There are two general ways of responding to this refusal to meet. The first is to respond, again, by letter. The letter summarizes the behaviors of concern which the team has developed (being careful to avoid diagnostic language or breaches of confidentiality: see Appendix A). It states the team's goal, or the school's decision regarding appropriate help (e.g., an alcohol/drug assessment, attending a support group, etc.). It also reminds parents that they have failed to participate in the school's attempt to help, and that the school and others have had to make decisions without their input. It then states the consequences of the student's current behavior, of his failure to change, and of the parent's unwillingness to support the referral for help. The letter concludes with an invitation to meet with the school staff to discuss these issues in more detail (which becomes the intervention session). If parents still refuse, whatever consequences the team has identified are then enacted.

Exploiting crises   Faced with an explicit refusal to meet, the school can also take advantage of other opportunities for meeting with parents. Many schools will schedule a formal reinstatement conference with the parents of a student who has been suspended from school. This reinstatement conference can provide an excellent opportunity for intervening as it is in response to a recent crisis. Exploiting other crises for intervention purposes is also possible: an arrest, a drug overdose, a suicide attempt, violence, or truancy. In addition, some parents are accustomed to attending meetings designed to assess their child's eligibility for special education programs. One of these sessions could become an intervention meeting if the concerns about the student's behaviors are serious enough, especially where the school has evidence of drug abuse. In other words, once the team is fully prepared for the intervention it must be ready to hold the meeting in response to events.

CHAPTER TWELVE

THE INTERVENTION MEETING

The previous chapters indicate that when the school develops a serious concern for a student's behavior, confronting parents is not the first thing to do—it is the last. The preparation steps outlined in the previous chapters are designed to empower both the intervention team and the process to reduce parent denial to the point where they can accede to the team's goal.

In addition to preparation, the success of structured interventions relies to a significant degree on team members' adherence to a structured agenda as much as possible. While detours will assuredly arise, knowing and agreeing to abide by a specific agenda always gives members something to return to. Effective parent interventions are characterized by their adherence to an agenda made up of the following seven steps:

⇨ 1. Introducing the meeting

⇨ 2. Sharing non-drug-specific data

⇨ 3. Sharing drug-specific data

⇨ 4. Stating the goal and asking for compliance

⇨ 5. Stating consequences when necessary

⇨ 6. Closing the meeting

⇨ 7. Debriefing

Members of the intervention team should gather in the meeting room a few minutes prior to the intervention. This assures that everyone on the team is present and that the meeting can begin as soon as parents join them. Meeting a few minutes in advance also allows the team to review the agenda one more time and to discuss anything that may have arisen since their last meeting. In general, team members should be seated in a circle when parents arrive (most interventionists recommend against meeting around a table). Following the moderator's greeting, parents will take the seats set aside for them.

1. INTRODUCING THE MEETING

In introducing the meeting the moderator greets parents and thanks them for coming, introduces the members of the intervention team, states the purpose of the meeting, and secures a commitment from all to abide by basic ground rules. A statement of purpose should include at least two points: first, the group is meeting out of *care and concern,* and second, it is meeting to share its concerns and *to collaborate with parents in finding a remedy.* The basic ground

Purpose, ground rules

rules of the meeting involve the *commitment to listen* and not to interrupt. The commitment to listen does not legislate the silence of parents; it does, however, give team members or the moderator something of which to remind parents (as well as team members) in the event that they begin to interrupt or depart from their order of presentation. While the commitment to listen is necessary, the moderator may wish to promise parents confidentiality—what is said in the meeting will not leave the meeting and no records of the meeting are kept—if she feels parents may be concerned.

While every moderator will have her own words, the following is an example of a brief introductory script:

> *(To Mary's parents:) Good morning. We are all glad you could come today. Before we start, let me make sure you know everyone here. On my left is (name), Mary's homeroom teacher. Next to her is (name), Mary's guidance counselor. You know (name), our principal (and so on).*
>
> *We are all here because we care about Mary and have become very concerned about some things which have been happening to her in recent weeks. We want to share some of these events with you and arrive together at a course of action which we think will help her and you.*
>
> *(To everyone) Before we begin, though, I am aware that we have only a short time to meet. I am concerned that everyone has a chance to speak and to be fully heard. Will everyone agree to wait their turn and not to interrupt?*

With her introductory remarks finished, the moderator can invite the first person on the team to being sharing data.

2. SHARING NON–DRUG–SPECIFIC DATA

 There are essentially four distinct types of data, based on whether is *objective* or *personal*, and whether it is *non-drug-specific* or *drug-specific*. The script differs only slightly for sharing either type. Recall that objective data consists of matters of record or other objective information (e.g., attendance patterns, classroom conduct data, a suspension for drug abuse in school, etc.) while personal data consists of events which the team member has witnessed and which has had some emotional impact upon her (see Chapter 7). Recall, also, that in determining the order, non-drug-specific data is shared first—whether objective or personal—and drug-specific data is shared last.

A simple script for sharing data includes the following:

❑ *A "care and concern" statement.* In her own words, and in language appropriate to her relationship to the student, the team member should begin with an "I care" statement. The "I care" statement should also include a brief mention of the student's strengths or something positive about her. It ends with a statement that recent behaviors have become cause for concern or worry.

❑ *Specific facts.* The team member shares at least three factual behaviors of concern, being careful to include the specific *date or occasion* and the *behavior of concern*. Important facts can include the student's attempts to correct her behavior that have failed. Personal data should also include the *harmful outcome*, how the team member *felt at the time*, and *what they did* at the time (see Worksheet 7.3).

❑ *'This isn't like her.'* Including language such as "This isn't like her," "This is not the student I used to know," or "I would like to see the happy Mary back" reinforces that the problem is not Mary but her behavior.

❑ *'I want her to get help.'* Recall that the need for the intervention is based on the student's need for formal help. The team member should avoid saying "I think she needs help," as this is likely to provoke a denial by parents. She should also avoid announcing the specific form of help (e.g., treatment, etc.) at this time.

Note that the 'specific facts' will vary depending on whether they are objective or personal, the latter including the team member's emotional response to the behavior and what she may have done to enable at the time. It is important for the team member to be economical in her data: brief, yet including the relevant concrete details. While it may be tempting to go on at length, with vivid descriptions and analysis, the team member should bear in mind that the longer she speaks, the less impactful on parents will her data be.

3. SHARING DRUG-SPECIFIC DATA

 In determining the order of presentation, the team will have placed those with drug-specific information after those with other facts. Ideally, objective alcohol/drug abuse information should also come before more personal data. Objective alcohol/drug data includes any information that the student is abusing alcohol or other drugs to any degree (simple kinds, amounts, and frequencies information—see Chapter 7), facts concerning drinking and driving or other alcohol/drug violations of the law, examples of the student's attempts to control her abuse, violations of abstinence contracts in a support group, etc.

If the team has evidence of chemical dependency it should be stated as such. This will usually be done by a school counselor, support group leader, SAP coordinator, or an alcohol/drug professional from the community. For example:

> *"We believe that any alcohol or other drug abuse is harmful for kids, and that abstinence is the goal. For some students, drug abuse progresses to chemical dependency or addiction. This is the most serious and life-threatening form of drug abuse. One of the reasons we are so worried and why we are holding this meeting is that we have evidence that Mary may be chemically dependent and in need of treatment. For example...."*

Friends, siblings, and other family members—those who have some degree of emotional investment in the student—typically have more personal drug-specific data and generally share their data last. It is not always possible to segregate objective and personal data neatly. Siblings, for example, may have relatively factual information about the student's drug abuse as well as personal experiences where they have been harmed by it. In any event, the personal experiences should follow any objective information.

Interruptions　It is during the data sharing that parents are most likely to interrupt with resistances—denials, challenges—rather than objections. The team member, if interrupted, responds with either silence or an acknowledging statement, and continues with her data. The moderator can also intervene in the process at this point, reminding parents of their commitment to listen. Another way of acknowledging the parents' resistance is for the moderator to ask at this point if they have seen or experienced *anything of concern to them* recently:

> *(Moderator:) "Even though we all agreed not to interrupt, I am aware that some of this is very painful for you to listen to. I am wondering if you have seen anything in Mary's behavior that has worried you, too, lately?"*

Following the parent's responses, whether they contribute information or not, the team member may resume where she left off in her data, or the next person in the order begins speaking.

4. STATING THE GOAL

After all of the team members have shared their data, the goal is announced. The moderator is often the logical choice to announce the goal, though anyone on the intervention team may be selected to do so. In many cases a school counselor or principal states the goal.

In stating the goal, the moderator summarizes briefly what the team has just said and states its unanimous recommendation. Following this statement parents must be explicitly asked "Will you...". Care should be taken not to ask parents what they think about all of this, or what they think should be done. The nature of the denial system will most often prevent them from knowing the appropriate course of action. Instead, with the denial system weakened by the intervention, the team exploits the emotional vulnerability of parents at this point and asks "Will you...".

For example:

> *"I know this has been difficult for you. This is not a step that we would take if we did not care about Mary and worry about the things we have seen. I also know that you, like most parents, sincerely want what is best for your child. One of the things we have learned is that, whether or not drug abuse is the cause of all of these concerns, it has to be ruled out or dealt with before anything else can improve. That is why we would like you to agree to take Mary to the Center for Drug Problems for a professional assessment and to follow their recommendations. Will you agree to make an appointment in the next two days?"* (Review Chapter 8 for other types of goals).

This, of course is the moment at which parents are most likely to react with objections or resistance. The team must be aware of any signs of the emotional surrender to the process which a "yes." Each objection or resistance the parent raises is responded to as rehearsed, followed by a restatement of the request to get help. As each objection is answered, parents come closer and closer to the open admission that they, too, have been deeply pained by their child's behavior and their powerlessness to understand or control it. Many interventions will end here with the parents' agreement with the goal.

5. STATING CONSEQUENCES

In some cases, however, parents will adamantly refuse to support the school's recommendation. The team should be aware of the temptation to argue, restate data or add additional facts, ask parents why they will not support the goal, etc. These strategies will have no impact on a clear refusal. Instead, it becomes necessary for the team to state its consequences for the student's failure to change or for the parents' refusal to support appropriate help. The consequences the team has prepared, then, are shared only if parents refuse to support the goal.

To the parents' refusal, the moderator or the person who has presented the goal responds:

> *"I am very sorry to hear that. It has, though, become clear to all of us that we cannot continue to allow Mary's behavior to continue. There are a number of consequences for her continuing behavior, starting today, which you need to know about..."*

Each member of the intervention team shares her consequences, usually speaking in the order in which data was shared. Parents' attention should be continually kept focussed on the decision to seek help. Thus, each team member can conclude her consequence statement with *"I really want her to get help."*

It is not possible to script the consequences segment rigidly. Every parent, every student, and every intervention will be different. The team and the moderator need to be continually alert for signs of parents' surrender, or willingness to seek help. As consequences are shared, the moderator may see an opportunity to interrupt and restate the goal and the "Will you...?" question.

Most parent refusals turn into compliance after consequences are shared. If reported appropriately, without anger, blame, or punishment, consequences convince parents of the seriousness and commitment of the team members. The consequences also tell parents that there will be no more tacit support by key persons in the student's life for the situation continuing as it has. And, even the most resistant parent is implicitly aware of the inevitability of the consequences.

6. CLOSING THE MEETING

Regardless of the outcome, appropriately closing the meeting requires there to be no "unfinished business." This is not the same as ensuring that everyone leave the meeting feeling good. The moderator's role is to make sure that everyone has said what they need to say in order to be able to leave. Effective closure entails acknowledging overtly what *has happened* and what *will happen next*. The closure statement by the moderator should appreciate people's participation and acknowledge the anxieties and risks which team members experienced by their presence. It should also recognize, again, the difficulty for the parents. Closing language also reinforces the message of care and concern.

Post-intervention meeting with parents

If parents have acceded to the team's recommendation, the moderator can acknowledge what happens next by inviting parents to meet immediately with the relevant member(s) of the intervention team to make necessary arrangements. At that time the school can seek signatures on release of information forms, can give parents information about the assessment agency and the admission process, etc. If the goal has involved the student's participation in an in-school support group, school staff can explain the group's requirements, parents' role in monitoring behavioral contracts, etc.

If parents have remained adamant in their refusal, the moderator summarizes the consequences briefly. It is helpful if parents can be given a written statement which spells out the consequences exactly and in some detail.

Finally, the moderator can ensure effective closure by *briefly* allowing the group one more round, inviting team members and parents to say anything else they need to in order to be able to leave.

7. DEBRIEFING

 Intervention team members, including those who were involved as preliminary team members, should meet relatively soon after the intervention to process the experience. The debriefing allows team members an additional depth of closure which would not be appropriate with parents present. Team members should be encouraged to discuss their feelings about what occurred and to identify those things which were difficult for them to see, hear, do, or say. If the team has encountered a refusal, the moderator/facilitator will find it useful to reaffirm the consequences which everyone has agreed to impose. Some may require laying out more specific plans for a course of action.

This is also an opportunity to discuss the process itself, from preparation to confrontation, examining what went particularly well and what might need to be changed in the future. If parents have agreed to the group's goal, those involved in helping parents to make arrangements will need to report back to the team the result of this post-intervention meeting. Everyone on the team, for example, will need to know who will follow-up on the goal and how they will know that it has been accomplished successfully.

Appendix A

Legal Issues

As school staff contemplate confrontations with parents on behalf of troubled students, legal issues arise in at least four areas: (1) liability arising due to the confrontation itself, (2) liability for the cost of treatment, (3) federal confidentiality regulations, and (4) parents' rights to inspect student records under the Family Rights and Privacy Act (FERPA).

Liability for Confronting

Perhaps in response to parents' past threats to sue, many school staff fear that a structured confrontation of the type outlined here will place them at legal risk. The fact is that such fears, though psychologically valid, are legally groundless. The simple fact of confronting parents with facts concerning their child's behaviors of concern does not place the school or the intervention participants at legal risk, so long as it is done without malice and with the best interests of the student and/or his family at heart.

Liability for Treatment Costs

A stronger concern arises around the liability for paying for the costs of assessment or treatment if the school makes a specific referral recommendation in these areas. As discussed in Chapter 8 (p. 56), in some states a school is held liable for treatment costs if it refers a student to a specific form of drug abuse treatment. In some states, however, a school may not be liable to pay if it offers a recommendation rather than a formal referral, and if it provides parents with a choice among several programs available in the community. Until the legal issues surrounding this issue have evolved further, it is wise for the school to consult with its own attorney and with its state health and education authorities for guidance.

FEDERAL CONFIDENTIALITY REGULATIONS

Federal confidentiality regulations (usually cited as 42 U.S.C § 290 dd-3 and § 290 ee-3; 42 C.F.R. Part 2) guarantee the privacy of clients (including students) receiving alcohol and drug abuse services. The restrictions forbid any such program from disclosing—without the student's prior written consent—any information that would identify the student as a client or as an alcohol or other drug abuser to anyone outside the program. Students are protected by the confidentiality regulations if they have applied for or have been provided services under the program. The confidentiality regulations specifically state that school-based substance abuse programs are covered by the confidentiality requirements. (For one detailed opinion on the application of confidentiality regulations to schools, see *Legal Issues for School-based Programs*, Legal Action Center, 153 Waverly Place, New York, NY 10014).

The confidentiality regulations can have an impact on the parent intervention process by prohibiting certain school staff from disclosing to parents or others, in the absence of the student's written consent, information that would identify the student as an alcohol or other drug abuser. And yet, this information may be crucial to the intervention process. How can the intervention team navigate through the confidentiality regulations and still conduct an appropriate and successful intervention?

Obtain Consent

The confidentiality regulations provide that information can be disclosed to third parties if the disclosure is explicitly consented to through a release of information (e.g., see Worksheet 8,2 on page 63). In the course of working with a student, the school staff should attempt to get a release of information signed by the student, specifically listing which types of information can be shared, with whom it can be shared, and for what purpose. In cases where a student is willing to seek assessment or treatment but parents are not, obtaining the release may not be a problem.

Re-examine Sources

The confidentiality regulations apply specifically to alcohol/drug abuse programs and to staff who have formal roles in the program that involve providing services such as assessment, counseling, treatment, or referral for treatment. In other words, there may be members of the intervention team who have alcohol/drug-specific data but who may not fall under the regulations. A classroom teacher, for example, who has no formal role in the drug abuse program, may have witnessed alcohol/drug specific behaviors in a student. This information may be shared with parents and with others on the intervention team without violating confidentiality regulations. Similarly, coaches, siblings, family members, peers, or others from the community may not be so constrained as well. School counselors, support group leaders, and others who may have formal roles in the school's substance abuse program may not be able to make unconsented drug-specific disclosures to parents.

Is the Student a "Client?"

Alcohol/drug-specific information may also be shared without permission if the student has not applied for or been given services by the program. If the intervention preparation process occurs before the student has been provided any alcohol/drug abuse services by the school, information uncovered during the intervention process may be able to be shared with parents without violating confidentiality requirements. In most cases, however, the decision to intervene will be validated by the history of the student's failure to change behavior in response to services such as counseling, support groups, etc.

Is the Alcohol/drug Abuse Data Necessary?

If it cannot obtain the student's consent, the intervention team may need to ask if it is necessary to share all of the alcohol/drug-specific information it has gathered. There may be those on the team who are not covered by the confidentiality regulations and who may shared their data, whereas others may not be able to. A decision may have to be made to proceed with the intervention while withholding some pieces of drug-specific data.

FERPA

While federal confidentiality regulations protect students' privacy, the Family Educational Rights and Privacy Act (20 U.S.C. § 1232g) gives parents of students under the age of 18 the right to inspect their child's educational records. A record, under the FERPA regulations, must be recorded and must be maintained by the educational institution. Informal notes and "memory joggers" that are not shared with others are generally not included.

Thus, FERPA regulations might be construed as permitting the intervention team to disclose certain information to parents if they formally request it and if the information is contained in formal records. Theoretically, the data collection worksheets could be considered as formal records rather than as personal notes. It may be possible for the intervention team to have parents sign a formal request to examine its records as a prelude to the intervention meeting.

CONCLUSION

There are clearly potential conflicts between the federal confidentiality regulations and the FERPA guidelines. The scope of the application of federal confidentiality regulations to school-based substance abuse programs is also still unclear to many. Much, for example, depends on how the school defines its "program," whether there is a well-defined "program," and the relationship of the intervention team or its members to the program. It is not the purpose of this appendix to provide specific legal advice or to interpret existing statutes, but rather to outline what appear to apparent pitfalls in disclosing to parents alcohol/drug-specific information concerning their child's need for help. In navigating between the extremes of the parents' right to know, the student's need for and resistance to help, and the school's obligations under the law, it is wise for schools to consult with their state agencies concerning advice on the applicability of the various regulations.

APPENDIX B

INTERVENING WITH A STUDENT

Chapters 4 through 12 outline a basic, proven technique for intervening with parents whose denial is preventing them from appreciating the nature, scope, and implications of their child's problem, and consequently from knowing about or taking steps to get appropriate help. Our focus in this book has been upon parents and on alcohol and other drug abuse.

If the basic process is well-understood, educators can become very creative at adapting it successfully to a host of other situations.

Recall, however, that the issue that this intervention process is designed to deal with is *denial*, not any specific problem or any specific person. Consequently, the basic preparation and confrontation steps can be adapted to many different troubling situations which educators face as they work with students and families. One could, for example, take the words "alcohol and other drug abuse" out of much of what has been said and substitute any other problem about which either students and/or their families have any degree of denial, and the process would be almost entirely the same. Similarly, one could substitute "student" for "parent" in the previous discussion and have an effective, workable process for dealing with students who are refusing to get help.

The intervention process which focuses on parents can often be the prerequisite for intervening with the student. As mentioned in Chapter 8, it is to some degree illegitimate to ask parents to admit to a treatment or assessment program a child over which they have no control. The *long-range goal* of the parent intervention may, indeed, be assessment or treatment for their student. The *short-range goal* may be for them to agree to participate in an intervention for their child.

Consider also the case, increasingly common, where one parent has been cooperative with the school but the other either refuses to get involved or has refused to support appropriate help in the past. The more cooperative parent becomes a member of the intervention team; the intervention process we have described can be useful in getting the denying parent to agree to either of the types of goals above.

In any event, adapting the intervention process to focussing on the troubled student can be relatively straightforward if the facilitator understands the basic principles behind it:

- Utilize a team of people who are meaningful to the student and who represent as many key segments of his life as possible.

- Educate members of the team in the nature of the problem and the nature of the intervention preparation and confrontation process

- Collect first-hand, concrete data about the student's behavior from people with personal experience with him.

- Insure that the team is united in an appropriate, realistic goal for the student. Make sure that the goal is not something he has to understand, agree with, or admit to. The only appropriate goal is to have the student agree to do something or go somewhere and follow through with what is recommended there.

- Make certain that team members have appropriate consequences for the student's failure to agree with the goal or to change his behavior—consequences which team members are truly committed to follow through with.

- Assist the team in anticipating the student's objections, resistances, and refusal to get help, so they do not unwittingly participate in his denial system.

- Prepare the team to follow a clear, concrete agenda for the confrontation meeting, which they have rehearsed.

Appendix C

TO THE FACILITATOR

The major factor that predicts the success of any structured intervention is the amount and quality of preparation. Are the data, goals, and consequences for the intervention meeting clear and appropriate? Are the team members emotionally prepared to intervene? Chapters 4 through 11 outline eight preparation steps essential to a successful intervention with parents.

The amount of time required to prepare intervention team members adequately will vary greatly, depending on the unique situation which each student and family presents, and on the previous background, training, and experience of all team members. There are a number of keys to preparing team members adequately in an economical period of time. First, the facilitator should himself understand the preparation process. Secondly, team members should be asked to do as much individual homework as possible on their own. Finally, *team* meetings should be utilized for *team work*. For example, it is inefficient to utilize a team meeting to have members start recalling and writing data: a more effective use of time is to have members bring their data to a meeting which is devoted to sharing and evaluating it—a group task.

The facilitator can orchestrate a successful parent intervention in four preparation meetings or less, each approximately one hour in length, by preparing team members for each session in advance and by combining several preparation tasks into each meeting.

Session One

The first meeting of the preliminary intervention team is typically devoted to physically assembling the team, explaining the decision to intervene, and orienting the team to the remaining preparation steps.

Preparation

Before convening the first team meeting the facilitator should accomplish a number of tasks:

Facilitator's checklist

❏ Gather or compile as much preliminary data as possible, consisting of "behaviors of concern," which legitimizes the need for a parent intervention. Be sure to include past attempts to deal with the student and/or parents which have not been successful.

❏ Identify potential preliminary team members, based on preliminary data or on informal discussions with school staff and others, according to the criteria in Chapter 5. The student assistance program Core Team process will often provide a vehicle for these preliminaries (see p. 28).

❏ Develop a list (see Worksheet 5.1, "Preliminary Intervention Team Roster") of potential team members.

❏ Contact potential team members in person or through a memo, inviting them to the first preparation meeting.

The Meeting

In introducing the first session the facilitator will:

Facilitator's checklist

❏ Introduce the session by reiterating the factors which have precipitated the concern and the decision to intervene.

❏ Explain that three more meetings will be held in order to prepare for a final intervention session with parents. Assure participants that their attendance at this session does not commit them to the remaining meetings, or to participating in the intervention itself. Emphasize, however, that participation in the intervention will require everyone to have participated in these preparation sessions.

❏ Introduce the current participants and provide a brief rationale for why each was invited.

❏ Describe briefly the tasks of the remaining three sessions.

❏ Explain his role in the remaining preparation steps.

Following the preliminaries, team members may have questions about the need to intervene, the process, their role, etc., which the facilitator should address.

Homework

In preparation for the next session, the facilitator will describe the collection of relevant intervention data, covering the following relevant points:

Facilitator's checklist

❏ The relationship of data to legitimacy and denial;

❏ The general characteristics of effective data (outlined in Chapter 7), which require it to be first-hand, detailed, specific behaviors of concern. A brief handout of these criteria can be very useful in guiding team members in generating their data.

❏ The types of alcohol/drug-specific information

❏ The nature of personal data

❏ The facilitator can supply team members with the relevant sample worksheets. Worksheet 7.1 (p. 48) is useful for collecting objective behaviors of concern by school staff; Worksheet 7.2 (p. 50) can be useful for family members and the student's peers; Worksheet 7.3 (p. 53) is useful for individuals who have direct, personal experiences with the student's alcohol/drug abuse.

❏ After responding to their questions, the facilitator should then direct team members to bring to the next session as many facts or as much information as they can gather or recollect which have a bearing on the student's unacceptable performance or behavior.

Session Two

The primary tasks of the next meeting include pooling intervention data and preparing the group to identify a goal and consequences.

Preparation

In preparation for the meeting, the facilitator may need to meet individually with those team members (especially peers or family members) who need help in deciding what they have seen or in being specific.

The Meeting

The first half of the meeting is devoted to having team members take turns reporting to the group three or four of the most significant facts or incidents which they have collected. It is most often useful not to allow other team members to interrupt with questions or comments until all have reported. Then incidents can be clarified and the data can be evaluated. While collecting and reviewing the data has a pragmatic significance for the eventual intervention, it also serves a number of purposes for the intervention team. First, since no single member has access to all the data, hearing it in its entirety serves to address whatever denial team members may have regarding the student's situation: things are deeper and wider than most have thought. Secondly, the reluctance of some team members to participate further can be reduced as they hear all of the facts. Pooling the data also tends to erode any doubts team members may have had about the effectiveness of the intervention with parents. After all of the data has been shared it will often be useful to allow the group to discuss briefly what they have heard.

The major function of the facilitator involves listening carefully to each fact as it is shared. When all of the data has been reported, he can assist the group in evaluating and critiquing the data along the following lines:

Facilitator's checklist

❑ Is the data appropriate (first-hand as opposed to rumors, generalizations, opinions, or hearsay?)

❑ Are the significant details present (e.g., the occasion, the drug abuse behavior, the harmful outcome, how the team member felt and reacted at the time, etc.)?

❑ Is the data brief? (E.g., during the intervention, long descriptions will detract from the impact of the facts on parents).

❑ Is there drug abuse-specific data?

❑ Is there data concerning evidence of chemical dependency?

❑ Is the language used by team members appropriate? In describing personal experiences with the student's drug abuse, care should be taken to avoid "loaded" adjectives such as "wasted," "blasted," "sloshed," "blitzed," etc., which will provoke parent defensiveness. The facilitator can suggest alternatives such as *"John had so much to drink that..."* or *"John was so intoxicated that..."*.

❑ Finally, is it going to be enough? Is this data likely to be maximally impactful for parents to hear? Are there any facts which people want to add? Are there other individuals who should be invited to take part?

As the data is evaluated and modified, team members can be encouraged to write it up in a final form that is appropriate for them. This list is what they will bring with them to the actual intervention session.

Pooling data in this way also amounts to an unofficial assessment. The group now has a much more complete picture of the nature and scope of the student's problem and perhaps even some idea concerning the implications for appropriate help. At this point, it is often possible to begin establishing a goal for the intervention meeting. Where alcohol and other drug abuse are involved, the ultimate goal will be abstinence. The group needs to be informed about the range of options that may help the student to achieve this goal: assessment or treatment, participation in a school-based support group, behavior contracting, etc. (see Chapter 8).

A member of the intervention team who has some specific background by training or experience in alcohol/drug abuse may recommend a specific goal. This may be member of the student assistance program's Core team or an alcohol/drug abuse specialist from the community. If time permits, the facilitator can ask the group if it will unanimously support a given goal. Team members are permitted to air divergent opinions or to ask questions about various options, for example. Ultimately, however, the decision must be unanimous. Sometimes the discussion of the goal takes place now, and a decision is postponed until the next meeting.

Homework

The next session will be devoted to reaching a consensus on an intervention goal for parents and on developing consequences for the student's failure to change or parents' failure to support the group's goal. The role of the facilitator at this stage is to educate the team about the nature of consequences, including the following (see Chapter 10):

Facilitator's checklist

❏   Why consequences are essential

❏   What are inappropriate consequences?

❏   What are appropriate consequences?

❏   What are the major types of consequences?

❏   What are some representative examples?

Team members are assigned to bring to the next session a written list of at least two or three specific consequences, stating what they will or will not do if the student fails to change his behavior or if the parents refuse to support the intervention goal. Team members usually find a brief handout, summarizing the criteria, above, useful.

Session Three

The next session combines finalizing the goal with arriving at a commitment to following through with consequences if necessary. Team members are also prepared for the final session, the rehearsal.

The Meeting

Before team members report their consequences, the facilitator makes sure that the team reaches a consensus on the goal.

Consequences will be shared with parents in the event that they refuse to support the group's goal. It is important that the facilitator prepare the group for this eventuality by stressing that the intervention is not guaranteed to work, and that the student cannot be allowed to continue on his present course.

Group members are invited to take turns reporting to the group the preliminary consequences they have identified.

The facilitator should invite group members to assist him in evaluating each others' consequences as they shared:

❏ Are you really willing to do that?
❏ Are you able to do that?
❏ Is that a natural/logical outcome of the student's or parents' behavior?
❏ Is it a confident assertion by the team member of his right to be healthy, happy, or safe?
❏ Is any aspect of the consequence enabling?
❏ Is the consequence individualized, in an "I" statement?
❏ Is the consequence an empty threat, a bargain or sacrifice, a punishment?

Since developing consequences is the most difficult part of the preparation process, members may not be able to identify accurate consequences by themselves. Team members should also be encouraged to suggest to each other what they could invoke as appropriate consequences. No consequence, however, is appropriate until it is thoroughly "owned" by the relevant team member.

When consequences are finalized, the facilitator can utilize Worksheet 10.1 ("Consequences Summary Sheet") to summarize them for himself, for the moderator's reference during the intervention meeting, and/or as the basis for a written statement of consequences to be given to parents.

Homework

Team members' "what if" questions can arise from the beginning. The facilitator may wish to respond to them briefly at the time, knowing that in Session Four they will be dealt with in detail. In preparation for the next session the facilitator should focus the team's attention on the forms that parents' objections or resistances may take. In preparing group members, he should:

Facilitator's checklist

❏ Educate the team on the difference between objections and resistance;

❏ Have team members bring to the next meeting a written list of what they predict parents' *objections* to the goal might be;

❏ Have team members bring to the next meeting a list of written *solutions* to each objection

The facilitator may wait until the next rehearsal session to have the team focus on parent resistance in detail. He can also prepare them to some degree in this session by:

Facilitator's checklist

❑   Explaining the nature of resistance, giving illustrative examples (e.g., see Chapter 9, pp. 66-71)

❑   Asking team members to bring to the next meeting a written list of the forms they anticipate parent resistance taking during the intervention.

❑   Describing what will happen during session four, the rehearsal;

❑   Asking the team for suggestions as to who should play the parts of the parents during the rehearsal.

Team members might find Worksheet 9.1, "Anticipating Denial," (p. 73) to be a helpful guide in preparing for the next session.

Session Four

This session is devoted to helping the team to identify and prepare responses to parents' objections and resistance, to practicing the intervention, and to planning how to convene parents.

Preparation

In preparing for the final preparation session, the facilitator can devote some thought to the practical details of the intervention, including the order of presentation, selecting and working with a moderator (if it is not to be himself), and anticipating any problems in getting parents to attend the intervention session.

The Meeting

The beginning of the session can be devoted to reviewing with team members their predictions concerning parent objections and resistance, based on the lists they bring with them. At this time, the facilitator/moderator can enlist the group in:

Facilitator's checklist

❑   Evaluating the viability of the solutions proposed for possible parent objections;

❑   Suggesting additional objections and brainstorming solutions to them;

❑   Reporting the forms they predict parent resistance may take;

❑   Discussing the general responses to resistance (Chapter 9) and suggesting appropriate responses for team members.

Prior to role playing the intervention meeting, the facilitator/moderator should next:

*Facilitator's
checklist*
☑

❑ Review with the group the rationale and his suggestions for an appropriate order of presenting data;

❑ Review the agenda for the intervention meeting and the rehearsal (see Chapter 11, p. 84);

❑ Review an appropriate script with which team members can present their data (see Chapter 12, pp. 89-90)

❑ Give some coaching to those who will play the roles of parents.

The role play should take the team all the way through the sharing of consequences and closure. As the role play progresses, the facilitator or moderator can be watching for key components of the intervention process:

*Facilitator's
checklist*
☑

❑ Is the meeting properly introduced?

❑ Are members following an appropriate script?

❑ Are members using appropriate language?

❑ Is the goal stated clearly?

❑ Are team members fluent in their response to objections?

❑ While the purpose of the rehearsal is to give team members a chance to practice the intervention agenda, it is also the most ideal way of identifying the various parent reactions which are likely to "hook" team members. As the role play unfolds, the moderator should be alert to these "hooks," interrupting the process from time to time to assist team members in identifying alternative ways of responding.

❑ Are team members clear in their statement of appropriate consequences?

❑ Is the meeting appropriately closed?

❑ Has anything happened which will be needlessly provocative of parents? What are some other ways of behaving?

The rehearsal can be processed in much the same way as the debriefing which will follow the actual intervention. Participants should be invited to share any feelings or observations they have, and any final concerns they have about the actual meeting should be addressed.

It would be ideal to schedule the rehearsal to immediately precede the actual intervention meeting but this is not always possible. At times the actual intervention will be scheduled in response to a crisis or some other circumstance. If this is the case, the end of the final preparation session should be devoted to informing the team about the circumstances which will precipitate the intervention.

REFERENCES

Anderson, Gary L. *When Chemicals Come to School: The Student Assistance Program Model.* 1988. Community Recovery Press. PO Box 20979, Greenfield, WI 53220.

Gorksi, Terrence T. "The Denial Process and Human Disease." Harvey, IL: Ingalls Memorial Hospital. [mimeograph]

McAuliffe, Robert M. and Mary Bosen McAuliffe. *The Essentials of Chemical Dependency.* Volume I. Minneapolis, MN: The American Chemical Dependency Society, 1975a.

_____. *Essentials for the Diagnosis of Chemical Dependency.* Volume II. Minneapolis, MN: The American Chemical Dependency Society, 1975b.

Schaefer, Dick. *Choices and Consequences.* 1987. Minneapolis: The Johnson Institute.

INDEX

To Reorder:

Intervening With Parents ($24.95), by Gary L. Anderson. A step-by-step guide for educators faced with resistant parents. Following its introduction to the nature of denial, confrontation, and intervention, this guide provides detailed guidelines for deciding when to intervene, assembling an intervention team, collecting relevant data, and structuring a successful intervention meeting with parents. Worksheets and sample forms lead the facilitator through the preparation process. A *must* resource for the student assistance program professional. 128 pages.

10 Steps for Preventing Student Relapse ($29.95), by Thomas J. Shiltz. A comprehensive guide to establishing processes, procedures, and services for students returning to school from chemical dependency treatment. This reference work contains an extensive discussion of relapse prevention information, with 45 supplements concerning how to deal with specific issues confronting the educator working with the recovering adolescent. Icons in the text refer to relevant exercises in the **Student Guide for Relapse Prevention** workbook. 196 pages.

Student Guide for Relapse Prevention ($6.95), by Thomas J. Shiltz. This workbook contains 43 exercises designed to assist recovering students working on various recovery tasks, from the re-entry to the school setting to the later stages of recovery. It contains sections on returning from treatment, each of the 12 Steps of AA, understanding relapse, tools and skills for growth, and relationships with others. It is an extremely useful workbook for educators, adolescent treatment staff, aftercare workers, and adolescents themselves. 84 pages.

When Chemicals Come to School: The Student Assistance Program Model. ($34.95), by Gary L. Anderson. This best-selling text, now in its eighth printing, is widely accepted as the "bible" for designing, implementing and operating student assistance programs. Its 477 pages contain sections on what student assistance programs are, on how to design a program, the place of support groups in an effective SAP, the process of implementation, and program maintenance. Over 60 "supplements" and worksheets assist educators in putting effective programs together. 477 pages.

ORDER FORM   ro

Ship to:

Name: _____
Organization: _____
Address: _____
City _____State _____ Zip _____

Bill to: (Purchase order #: _____)

Name: _____
Organization: _____
Address: _____
City _____State _____ Zip _____

Quantity	Title	Price Each	Shipping ($2.50 each)	Total
	Intervening With Parents, *Anderson*	$24.95		
	10 Steps for Preventing Student Relapse, *Shiltz*	$29.95		
	Student Guide for Relapse Prevention, *Shiltz*	$6.95		
	When Chemicals Come to School, *Anderson*	$34.95		

Total for Order: [ ]

Make Checks payable to "Community Recovery Press" and mail to:

Community Recovery Press
PO Box 20979
Greenfield, WI 53220

or FAX your order to:
(414) 679-0384